THE
NEW WEB TYPOGRAPHY
CREATE A VISUAL HIERARCHY WITH RESPONSIVE WEB DESIGN

THE
NEW WEB TYPOGRAPHY
CREATE A VISUAL HIERARCHY WITH RESPONSIVE WEB DESIGN

STEPHEN BOSS
JASON CRANFORD TEAGUE

CRC Press
Taylor & Francis Group
Boca Raton London New York

CRC Press is an imprint of the
Taylor & Francis Group, an **informa** business

A CHAPMAN & HALL BOOK

CRC Press
Taylor & Francis Group
6000 Broken Sound Parkway NW, Suite 300
Boca Raton, FL 33487-2742

Printed on acid-free paper
Version Date: 20160519

International Standard Book Number-13: 978-1-138-78139-9 (Paperback)

Visit the Taylor & Francis Web site at
http://www.taylorandfrancis.com

and the CRC Press Web site at
http://www.crcpress.com

TABLE OF CONTENTS

INTRODUCTION

... When it is a good design, the reader has to feel comfortable because the letter is both banal and beautiful.

Adrian Frutiger

You are a typographer. If you type anything on a computer, you have committed an act of typography. You have set letterforms that will aid in the communication of a written message. You may not get ink on your thumbs, or have to stress out about kerning, leading, and tracking, but you have set type. Everyone is a typographer now, but how good is up to you.

Typography is the practice of arranging type within a design. This includes not only the selection of a typeface, but also the size, spacing, color, and styles of type. Typography also deals with the design of type on the page and its interaction with other elements such as photos, illustrations, and interface. The treatment of the text can be every bit as important to the message as the actual words themselves.

abcdefghijklmnopqrstuvwxyz

EMBAUHAUS

WHAT IS "GOOD" TYPOGRAPHY?

DO NOT DESIGN BY DEFAULT

Typography is the architecture that supports all visual communications, from print to wayfinding, and, of course, the Web. Designers create type systems to build a visual hierarchy, to create the order and flow needed to guide users through their experience. These elements can include headlines, body copy, subheads, navigation, sidebars and more. You should always develop your own design voice, rather than using prebuilt templates.

GIVE YOUR TEXT A VOICE

Developing your site's typographical voice will be similar to casting a chorus: you'll want tenors, bass, sopranos, and baritones. Each of these has a unique timbre and all blend together to make wonderful music. Your type selections achieve the same goal. The weight and style of your headlines can make them rich and attention grabbing, while a simple geometric typeface for your body copy can be quite subtle. Use the cards on this page to visualize what voice a typeface can bring to your design.

Slab Serif

OFTEN HEAVY AND IMPOSING—A DIRECT AND EVOLVED TRANSITIONAL FORM

Archer Pro Medium
ABCDEFGHIJKLMNOPQRSTUVWXYZ
abcdefghijklmnopqrstuvwxyz
1234567890

Serif

DRIVEN BY TRADITIONAL VIRTUES—PROVIDING HOPE WHEN ALL ELSE FAILS

Adobe Caslon Regular
ABCDEFGHIJKLMNOPQRSTUVWXYZ
abcdefghijklmnopqrstuvwxyz
1234567890

Sans Serif

ASSERTIVE AND FAMILIAR—ENFORCING STRUCTURE AND AUTHORITY

Gotham Book
ABCDEFGHIJKLMNOPQRSTUVWXYZ
abcdefghijklmnopqrstuvwxyz
1234567890

Didone

SMART BUT STYLISH—INFLUENTIAL WITH ITS CURVES WHILE DECEPTIVE IN WEIGHT

Bodoni Roman
ABCDEFGHIJKLMNOPQRSTUVWXYZ
abcdefghijklmnopqrstuvwxyz
1234567890

Blackletter

OF ANCIENT ORIGINS—COMBINING BOTH DRAMATIC AND ELABORATE CHARACTERISTICS

Fette Fraktur
ABCDEFGHIJKLMNOPQRSTUVWXYZ
abcdefghijklmnopqrstuvwxyz
1234567890

DISPLAY

DISTINCT BUT UNIFIED—EACH CONTAINING A SEPARATE PERSONALITY AND POWER!

SOPRANO

MEZZO SOPRANO

TENOR

BARITONE

BASS

OVERVIEW

1

Never mistake legibility for communication

David Carson

Font selection is more than a cosmetic choice, it is a push and pull of harmonies and tensions that create a robust page, one that pulls the reader into your narrative. Similar to how a wine buff looks for depth of flavor, a reader wants to have their taste buds tickled. This can be achieved in many ways. A minimalist style, one that follows the KISS theory (Keep it Simple, Stupid) is safe; a classical look is dignified; a contemporary font can be dynamic.

The project will more than likely help you decide which direction to take, and the overall tone of graphics should suit the subject. Please consider the following tips on creating your font palette to ensure quick download times and overall aesthetics.

abcdefghijklmnopqrstuvwxyz

CONSOLAS

CHOOSING THE RIGHT TYPEFACE

When you only had 10 fonts, choosing one from the list was easy. Now that you have dozens of Web-safe fonts, and can link to any font that is licensed for Web downloading, your horizons are much broader. This new power, though, comes with the responsibility of having to be thoughtful in your choices. The exact type you choose should depend on several factors.

ESTABLISH A TYPOGRAPHIC VOICE

Choose your typeface to reflect the mood and demeanor of the message your Web site is meant to reflect. If the site is meant to be upbeat and happy, choose fonts with a playful look to them. If the site is meant to be professional and serious, choose clean simple fonts.

I once worked with a writer who published a daily advice column. She insisted, despite my protests, to publish her column in Comic-sans, a font that is generally ridiculed by typographers. However, I quickly realized that this font "spoke" to her audience in a relaxed informal tone that no other available font could have achieved. She was actually using the available typeface to better communicate her message.

We now have a much wider selection of fonts to choose from, so choose those that best serve the content's message. It's important that you define the voice you are trying to achieve, and then choose typefaces accordingly.

USE THE RIGHT FONTS IN THE RIGHT PLACES

A consequence of designers having ready access to more than just a handful of fonts is that we will likely see an explosion of bad typography. We've all seen inappropriate fonts on bank mailers and restaurant menus. Something similar happened early in Web design, when designers, used to the color limitations of print design, went a little bit overboard when they could use all and any colors in a single design. It is important with Web typography, as with any design, to always have a purpose for your typeface choices.

For example, in this book, I wanted to create a balance between the past and the future. All body copy is set in the Perpetua font family, which is also a Web-safe font. Titles and auxiliary content—like captions and sidebars—are set in the sans-serif typeface Museo, a free font you can use with `@font-linking` in a Web page. I chose these fonts because not only do they look good together—contrasting serif and sans-serif—but I also wanted to put my money where my mouth is by using typefaces that can be set both in print and in Web sites. The one typeface exception I made was for text used to display computer code, which is traditionally monospace, so I used Consolas.

If you are new to typography or design, limit yourself to a single font, leveraging its weights and styles and varying colors to create contrast.

BUILDING A FLUID FONT STACK

In Chapter 3, we explore the many ways to find typefaces for use in your Web designs. One of the prime tenets of fluid Web typography, is that things change, and you cannot be assured that the first font you choose is the one the end user reads your text in. There are many variables that can contribute to this uncertainty, but the solution is to be prepared by creating a fluid font stack with back-up fonts.

It is important, however, when putting the font stack together, to choose fonts that not only look similar but behave similarly on the page. Here are a few of the most important considerations.

FIND SCREEN-FRIENDLY FONTS FOR BODY COPY

Although you may have a candy store of fonts to choose from, some will be more legible at body copy sizes (16 px or below) than others. Two factors to consider with the legibility of a font are its x-height and letter spacing. A font with a taller x-height will generally be easier to read on the screen. Additionally, if you can find fonts that are slightly spaced apart, they will not clash with each other on the screen. If you need to, add a small amount of letter spacing or word spacing to headlines or body text.

USE FONTS WITH SIMILAR WIDTHS AND KERNING

Because headlines generally have a confined height—you don't want the headline to take up more than a certain vertical space in the design—choosing fonts with similar widths will ensure that one font will not take up much more space than any of the fall-backs.

Body copy may need to occupy a specific column width for readability, so choosing typefaces with similar widths and kerning will ensure that one does not take more vertical space than any of the alternatives.

Test your fonts by placing them one after another, comparing lengths (for headlines) and heights (for body copy). There is a certain amount of variation that can occur, but you don't want any font to be off from the other by more than 2 em over the width of the line.

MAKE SURE THAT A TYPEFACE INCLUDES ALL OF THE WEIGHTS AND STYLES YOU NEED

Although there are ways to style around missing font styles, you should make sure that if you are using the bold, italics, and/or oblique version of a typeface in your design, that the typeface supports these styles. Otherwise, the browser will likely synthesize them, which rarely looks good.

One way around this is to actually specify different typefaces or different styles rather than bold or italics. For example, rather than using a heavier font for the bold or strong tags, you could set font weight to normal and use all caps or small caps.

```
b, strong {

    font-weight: normal;
```

Use this technique sparingly, as it can create a strong typographic voice that may not be desired.

DOWNLOAD FONTS AS NEEDED, BUT CONSIDER DOWNLOAD TIMES

Although downloading fonts allows you to add typefaces without images, you are still downloading files which can slow down your Web site. Check the list of Web-safe fonts first to see whether one of those meets your needs before resorting to the download. However, you will always want to put your linked fonts first, since whether you use them or not, the file is still downloaded.

INCLUDE WEB-SAFE, CORE, AND GENERIC FONT FAMILY BACK-UPS

Include a list of multiple fonts, starting with linked fonts, then Web-safe fonts, then core Web fonts, and finally a generic font family. This will ensure that the fonts you most want to be used are tried first, and then the fall-backs are tried all the way down to the default generic font the browser has on hand. Obviously, you can include as many different font families of each type as desired.

grotesque

CRIPT
ONOSPACE
UMANIST
ETRO

X CAP
HEIGHT

GEOMETRIC
FIXED WIDTH
BASE

TYPE BASICS

2

Electric means of moving
of information are
altering our typographic
culture as sharply as
print modified medieval
manuscript and scholastic
culture.

Marshall McLuhan
Understanding Media

Letter forms should always be at the service of the message being delivered. An honest understanding of what typography can and cannot do is essential to delivering that message.

Although every character and symbol—or glyph—in a typeface repertoire is unique, they share certain characteristics in common, and we can use these characteristics to better describe and understand how type works.

The anatomy lesson presented in this chapter will help give you the language you need to talk about and describe different fonts as well as understand their uses and strengths. Using fonts is more than simply choosing the one that looks the best to you, and invloves finding fonts that are as easy to read and scan in a given situation, while also providing a visual message in line with the text.

Glyph Lolly2012
• The visual representations of a single character or symbol within a font, distinguishable from all other characters in that set.

abcdefghijklmnopqrstuvwxyz
UNIBODY REGULAR

WHAT IS A GLYPH?

Consider the capital letter "A". Its two diagonal lines at an oblique angle connect at the top with a crossbar between them. Those are the intrinsic characteristics of the letter, what makes it an "A" and not a "B" or even an "a". And yet, even within these simple characteristics, there are an infinite number of possibilities.

A glyph is the generic term used to refer to any unique character within a font. It is a specific shape for an alphanumeric or other symbol. A font's repertoire is simply the glyphs that are included within the particular font. It is important to remember that not every font will include a specimen of every glyph. Also known as a font's repertoire or character range, every glyph in the font is in order for the encoding scheme. The term "character set" is often used synonymously with "character encoding."

Adobe Illustrator includes a glyph pallet which allows you to select any glyph from the font's repertoire.

WHAT IS A FONT?

Typeface • A collection of glyphs (numbers, letters, symbols and punctuation marks) as a set.

Font • A collection of glyphs with a specific weight, style, variant and/or stretch.

Alegreya Regular
Alegreya Bold
Alegreya Italic
Alegreya Bold Italic

The typeface is Alegreya. The fonts are Alegreya Regular, Alegreya Bold, Alegreya Italic, and Alegreya Bold Italic.

A font can be many different things, depending on the context of its use—or misuse. Although seemingly a matter of semantics, it's important to understand the distinction between a font and a typeface.

IS IT A FONT OR A TYPEFACE?

The terms "typeface" and "font" are commonly used synonymously although they are not the same. A typeface is a collection of glyphs (numbers, letters, symbols and punctuation marks) as a set. Typefaces might include a number of different weights and styles. For example, Alegreya is a typeface that includes regular, bold, italic, and bold italic. Typefaces are also commonly referred to as font families or type families.

A font, on the other hand, is a collection of glyphs with a specific weight, style, variant and/or stretch, for example, Alegreya Bold.

In Web design, the term "font family" is commonly used to distinguish from the more specific font term. However, the fact remains that the font term is commonly used when font family or typeface is what is meant. Since the misuse is so pervasive and the distinction slightly esoteric for common use, I'm not going to try and play the font police.

WHAT IS WEB TYPOGRAPHY?

HTML + CSS + *JavaScript* = Web Typography

Web typography is the practice of typography applied to text marked up using the Hypertext Markup Language (HTML) and styled using Cascading Style Sheets (CSS), both of which are standards defined by the World Wide Web Consortium (W3C). Occasionally, JavaScript (JS) will also be added into the mix to programmatically adjust styles that would otherwise be tedious to do by hand or to dynamically change styles for better transitions and user interaction.

HTML • Markup language used to structure Web pages.

CSS • Style sheet language used to design Web pages.

JS • Scripting language used to add interactivity to Web pages.

The World Wide Web Consortium (W3C; w3.org) sets the standards we use to design Web pages.

Text in an image is bitmapped, so it cannot be re-sized without the anti-aliasing pixels becoming obvious and losing fidelity.

Text in flash might be vector, but is not HTML or CSS.

Although commonly displayed using Web browsers, the principles of Web typography can be applied anywhere that text is so rendered, such as e-mail, instant messaging, and Web-enabled widgets and applications.

What Web Typography is **not**:

» *NOT Text in Images*: Text can be rendered in an image and will often need to be considered as part of the overall page's typography. However, it is not true Web text and cannot be selected or edited outside the image and lacks the ability to be re-sized without losing image fidelity.

» *NOT Text in Flash*: Text in an Adobe Flash "movie" is vector based text that can be displayed in many Web browsers with the appropriate plug-in. However, Flash does not use standard HTML to display the text and does not work on many tablet and mobile devices, making it a poor choice for modern user interface design.

Fidelity • The degree of exactness with which something is copied, reproduced, or re-sized.

BITMAP VS. VECTOR

There are two methods for how graphics (including glyphs) are stored to be rendered on a computer screen: bitmap and vector.

BITMAP

Bitmap images use a grid of pixels—like tiny mosaic tiles—that fool the eye into seeing one contiguous image. If you enlarge a bit map image, you will lose fidelity, and the image looks blurred and distorted.

All type on the screen and in print is eventually translated into bitmap for output, using a process called rasterisation. To further fool the eye, pixels at the edges are lighter color to blend with the background in a process called anti-aliasing, which creates the illusion of sharper edges, and font hinting is used to better refine anti-aliased text for display.

VECTOR

Vector images use mathematical formulas to store outlines and color fill of images and fonts. Although not as versatile for detailed images as bitmap graphics, vector graphics can be scaled as large as desired without losing fidelity.

Modern font files are stored in a vector format, allowing the characters to be scaled as large as you desire, although not all fonts are designed to be displayed at all sizes.

A BRIEF HISTORY OF WEB TYPOGRAPHY

By the time Tim Berners-Lee conceived of the World Wide Web in the early 1990s, computer operating systems were already evolving from the command line prompt to graphic interfaces, with type going from simple monospace fonts to more modern typefaces. The Hypertext Mark-up Language (HTML) included several typographic "tags" to specify paragraphs, headings, lists, glossary terms, and a few other styles no longer in use.

HTML 2.0, released in 1995, included tags for bold and italics and many browsers added their own tags including font and other typographic style tags. However, the limitations of tags for style were quickly recognized as diminishing the flexibility and extensibility of documents.

World Wide Web

The WorldWideWeb (W3) is a wide-area hypermedia information retrieval initiative aiming to give universal access to a large universe of documents.

Everything there is online about W3 is linked directly or indirectly to this document, including an executive summary of the project, Mailing lists , Policy , November's W3 news , Frequently Asked Questions .

What's out there?
    Pointers to the world's online information, subjects , W3 servers, etc.
Help
    on the browser you are using
Software Products
    A list of W3 project components and their current state. (e.g. Line Mode ,X11 Viola ,
    NeXTStep , Servers , Tools , Mail robot , Library)
Technical
    Details of protocols, formats, program internals etc
Bibliography
    Paper documentation on W3 and references.
People
    A list of some people involved in the project.
History
    A summary of the history of the project.
How can I help ?

A reproduction of the first Webpage by Tim Berners-Lee from 1989. A lot has changed about the technology since those early days, but one thing that didn't change for almost 20 years was the ability to use specific fonts.

To take the burden of styling documents off HTML—which was originally intended only as a way of specifying content use and not appearance in 1994, Bert Bos and Håkon Wium Lie worked on a language that would eventually become CSS. CSS defines the appearance of content that had been marked-up using HTML.

Although slow to be adopted, today CSS is considered as important as HTML in the creation of professional Web pages, in part because of its typographic control. CSS allows control over font weight, font styles such as italic, text spacing, and text decoration. It even allows the designer to specify font families including the download of particular font files. At least in theory.

Images have, obviously, been easy to download almost since the conception of the Web. Although we primarily use GIF, JPEG, and PNG formats, many browsers support EPS, TIFF, and BMP. So if images are so easy to download, what's the hang-up with fonts?

The most common digital font file formats in use today are TrueType Fonts (TTFs) and OpenType Fonts (OTFs), and if you look at your font catalogue, it's likely that most of your fonts are in one of these formats, with some possibly in Post Script. However, these formats lack digital rights management (DRM), meaning that any-one can use them and share their files whether they paid for them or not. Primarily for this reason, the browser manufacturers did not support fonts that require a license.

One exception was Microsoft's Internet Explorer, which has supported the embedded open type format (EOT) since the late 1990s. However, it's rarely seen in Web design, partially because it required that you go through a difficult ordeal to convert exist-

Core Web Fonts •

Andale Mono

Arial

Arial Black

Comic Sans MS

Courier New

Georgia

Impact

Times New Roman

Trebuchet MS

Webfonts • Any font that can be downloaded from a server and used in a Web design created using HTML and CSS.

ing fonts to the new format, but mostly because no other browsers could support it.

For the first 15 years of the Web's history, typography was excruciatingly limited due to almost no choice of typefaces. At first you had no control over the typeface used, then you could set a few generic styles, and finally, you could set the typeface name, but were essentially limited to the fonts installed on the end-users computer, only 10 Web safe-fonts which you could count on being available and only 5 of which were really of general use.

And that's where Web typography stalled for nearly 10 years—you could download fonts, but common font formats were unsupported and so designers relied on the Core Web Fonts that are almost guaranteed to be pre-installed on all computers running the Mac and Windows operating systems.

In 2008, Web browsers first began to support Webfonts, allowing fonts to be downloaded and used in a Web design regardless of what the user has pre-installed. At first, these fonts were all locally served, that is, the font files were on the same server as the HTML and CSS files using them. However, there were very few fonts that were licensed to be used as Webfonts.

There were places that you could download fonts for free or for a price that included the correct licenses, but many used services like Fontsquirrel to convert fonts they already possessed, not realizing that this was a violation of the end user license agreement (EULA).

Firefox did not allow fonts to be used from remote servers (cross-domain) without some additional server-see code. Firefox intentionally blocks fonts from different domains to prevent just anyone from being able to use the fonts on a server which is likely a violation of the fonts end user license agreement.

However, serving Webfonts, overcoming the technical limitations of Firefox, and making sure that the licensing was all in order were often daunting. As a result, there quickly developed services which served Webfonts from their own remote servers. These Webfont service ureaus (WFSBs) have grown in popularity, as they take a lot of the guesswork out of licensing fonts and ensure maximum cross-browser compatibility.

This all changed in 2008 when Apple released a version of its Safari Web browser that supported OpenType and TrueType fonts. This opened the flood gates and by 2009, Mozilla Firefox and Google Chrome were all supporting downloadable Web fonts. Of course, Internet Explorer had been supporting embedded opentype font (EOT) format for years, and work-arounds were quickly discovered that allowed developers to deliver Webfonts that worked on every major browser.

Even better, a new format—the Web Open Font Format (WOFF)—was developed that provided greater security for font creators from having their fonts used without a license. The standard was quickly adapted, and by 2013 had been adapted by every major browser and most mobile devices.

THE FUTURE OF WEB TYPOGRAPHY

In 2009 W3C started a new working group expressly to address the issues of Web fonts, separate from the CSS Working Group.

The Fonts Working Group (http://www.w3.org/Fonts/WG/) mission is to:

> *...allow wider use of fonts on the Web by identifying a font format that can be supported by all user agents, balancing font vendor concerns with the needs of authors and users and the simplicity of implementation.*
>
> *— From the Fonts Work Group Charter*
> *w3.org/2009/03/fonts-wg-charter*

Since 2009, the group has been working to establish a new and open standard, the Web OpenFont Format (WOFF) that will be used in place of the older standards. If you want to enter the fray yourself, subscribe to the W3C Web Fonts Public Mailing List if you dare (www-font-request@w3.org).

In addition to the fonts working group, the CSS Working Group continues to work on font and text properties, planning on further expanding the features, especially around taking advantage of open type font features and finally introducing real kerning.

UNDERSTANDING TYPE ON THE WEB

Web typography grew out of the larger field of digital typography that developed with the advent and growth of digital computers. Digital typography rose with the popularity of the personal computer in the 1980s, and eventually completely replaced analog type. However, it was not until the late 2000s that type on the Web went from being a curiosity to status as an actual discipline in and of itself.

WHAT IS A WEBFONT?

Webfonts are simply font files that can be used to display text in HTML. These font files are loaded from a Web server using the CSS *@font-face* rule and then included within a standard font stack using the *font* or *font-name* properties.

Although this may seem simple, it took years before font makers changed their EULAs to allow their work to be used on the Web, and, as a result browser manufacturers did not support any of the common font file formats.

The term Webfont was initially written as two words, but as these fonts gained in popularity, they have been increasingly combined into a single word, similar to Website.

EULA • End user Llicense agreement that specifies how a particular piece of software—such as a font—can and cannot be used by the owner.

notice the space

Webfont or Web font

WEBFONT FILE FORMATS

Fonts are actually small programs that tell the computer how to display characters. There are several formats in which fonts are commonly used with most computers.

TRUETYPE (.TTF)

TrueType fonts are outline-based fonts that contain all of the font data in a single file as opposed to PostScript Type 1 Fonts, which required multiple files. In Mac OS X, you might also encounter DFONT(.dfont) files which are TrueType files that have been converted from the older Mac OS9 operating system.

OPENTYPE (.OTF)

OpenType fonts are an extension of the TrueType format that includes more typographic control as well as allowing for older PosScript Type 1 fonts to be converted.

OpenType fonts (and WOFF fonts using open type) offer several features above and beyond TrueType. OpenType files can contain up to 65,535 characters or glyphs. This allows for multi-language support as well as advanced typographic features such as ligatures, figure styles, fractions, stylistic alternates, swashes, small caps, ornaments, borders, and so on. All these extras can live in one file instead of many.

A single OpenType file contains all the information required for a typeface style: metrics, kerning, outline, hints, and bitmaps.

POSTSCRIPT TYPE 1 FONTS

PostScript Type 1 is an older file format that is gradually being phased out in favor of OpenType. Two files are required for Type 1 fonts: the first with the actual outline information (.pfb on Windows and .lwfn on Mac), the other with metric data about the font, such as kerning (.pfm on windows and .fond on Mac).

SCALABLE VECTOR GRAPHIC (.SVG)

Fonts using the SVG format are glyphs recorded using the Web's standard vector format. These files tend to be larger than other font formats, but were often the only formats available in older mobile platforms before WOFF was widely adapted.

EMBEDDED OPEN TYPE (.EOT)

The EOT was developed as a proprietary format in the late 1990s to allow for safe downloadable Webfonts. At the time, though, Netscape (Internet Explorer's chief browser competition) created its own proprietary format, that was not widely adapted. EOT was all but forgotten until about 2008, when a Webfont solution was needed so that Internet Explorer could display Webfonts.

WEB OPEN FONT FORMAT (.WOFF)

The WOFF format was quickly developed in 2009 to respond to the quick adoption of less secure formats in Web browsers. WOFF is a container (wrapper) for fonts in other formats, but provides font metadata and private-use data separately from the font to allow creators to prevent it from being installed as a system font by the end user. Although the other formats work as Webfonts, WOFF is quickly rising as the standard, and other formats will likely be phased out.

WEBFONT COMPATIBILITY

Every major Web browser in use today supports some version of Webfonts. Although older versions of Internet Explorer rely on the EOT format, this still means that Webfonts will properly display, even back to Version 4 from the 1990s.

Even better, all newer versions of Web browsers support the WOFF format, which means that soon we'll only need to rely on that one format. Still, for backwards compatibility, I highly recommend including all four file types to ensure maximum cross browser compatibility.

Although there are plenty of older mobile devices in use around the world, the vast majority use mobile versions of Safari, Chrome, or Internet Explorer, all of which support Webfonts as well.

The tables on the next page show a compatibility chart for the different major browsers—Internet Explorer, Firefox, Safari, Chrome, and Opera—for both desktop/laptop and tablet/mobile versions, with the first supported version indicated to the right of the check mark.

DESKTOP/LAPTOP BROWSERS

	IE	Firefox	Safari	Chrome	Opera
EOT	✔ 4				
TTF/OTF		✔ 3.5	✔ 3.1		✔ 10
SVG			✔ 3.1	✔ 3	✔ 10
WOFF	✔ 9	✔ 3.6	✔ 5.1	✔ 5	✔ 11

TABLET/MOBILE BROWSERS

	IE	Firefox	Safari	Chrome	Opera
TTF/OTF		✔ 3.5	✔ 4.2	✔ 2.2	
SVG				✔ 3.1	
WOFF	✔ 10	✔ 3.6	✔ 5	✔ 4.4	✔ 11

FONT ANTI-ALIASING

Most screens still have a substantially lower resolution than the printed page. A computer screen is composed of a series of tiny squares (pixels) that combine to make everything from a photograph to a letter.

While print has a resolution of 144 dpi (dots per inch) or higher—usually at least 300 dpi for high-quality printing—computer screens most commonly have a resolution of 72 dpi or 96 dpi. These lower resolutions mean that characters on the computer screen tend to look rough and blocky at the edges, with the pixels evident to the naked eye.

To compensate and increase legibility and readability of text, most operating systems use a process called anti-aliasing, which adds transparent pixels to the edges of letters, producing the optical illusion that the edges of the text are smooth.

On the Mac, anti-aliasing is called Core Text smoothing and is controlled in the Appearance control panel. In Windows, the technology is called ClearType and is controlled in the Display Control Panel. While font smoothing is turned on by default on the Mac, it was not in Windows until Vista was developed.

Many browsers render type using the operating systems rendering engine to anti-alias type. But not all OSs are created equal in that regard. Whereas the Mac consistently uses its Core Text system, Windows machines may be using different anti-aliasing methods, depending on the user preference or installed software.

MAC OS X: ALL BROWSERS

All Web browsers running on the Mac use the system default text rendering engine—Core Text —and OS font smoothing settings. There are no browser preferences that affect the way type is anti-aliased. The upshot is that, type will look consistent on Macs.

WINDOWS: FIREFOX, CHROME, SAFARI, OPERA, AND IE6

Firefox, Chrome, Safari, Opera, and IE6 use the system default text rendering engine and OS font smoothing settings, meaning that the fonts should render consistently, although generally not as smoothly as on a Mac. Windows 7 and Windows Vista use ClearType sub-pixel anti-aliasing enabled by default, but Windows XP uses standard gray-scale anti-aliasing.

WINDOWS: IE7 & 8

IE7 overrides the default OS font smoothing setting with a preference called "Always use ClearType for HTML". It is enabled by default, which means that IE7 users will usually see type that is anti-aliased with ClearType—even if they are using Windows XP or have explicitly chosen standard font smoothing in their OS settings.

IE8 has the preference enabled by default. The difference is that when IE8 is installed, it forces the OS font smoothing setting to ClearType sub-pixel anti-aliasing.

WINDOWS: IE9 AND FIREFOX

IE9 and Firefox (where IE9 is installed) use Microsoft's DirectWrite text rendering engine, which is a much cleaner anti-aliasing engine than ClearType.

ANATOMY OF A CHARACTER

The baseline is an implied foundation to which the bottom of most type is aligned. It is generally a continuous horizontal line that runs the width of a column of text, breaking only when the right edge is reached, and then continuing on the next line of text.

The cap height is the distance from the baseline to the topmost reach of capital letters in a font, while the x-height is the distance from the baseline and the lower-case letter x in a font. The implied line created by the x-height and running parallel to the baseline

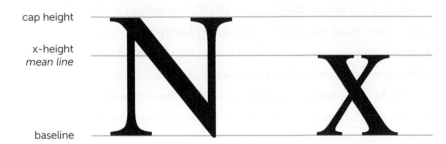

cap height

x-height
mean line

baseline

is called the mean line which is also, generally, the height of most lower case letters in the font.

The cap height and x-height can both vary greatly from font to font, depending on the needs of the designer, but both attributes

times　　rockwell　　georgia　　helvetica　　monaco

are important to take into consideration when we talk about choosing the best fonts in chapter 4.

WHAT TO LOOK AT WHEN CLASSIFYING A FONT

Typefaces can come in a seemingly infinite variety of shapes and sizes, but we typically look at a few features to evaluate most fonts for classifications. Serif brackets are the shapes of the embellishments in serifed fonts. Stroke curve is the amount of curvature in a character's stroke. Stroke slant is the angle of the simulated strokes used to create the letter form. Stroke weight is the overall thickness of the simulated stroke for a particular font. Stroke contrast is the variation between thick and thin in a single font's stroke weight. Counter size is the amount of negative space within the loops of enclosed letter forms such as the "a", "B", and "g".

SERIF & SANS-SERIF

Serifs are projections that extend from the main strokes of the characters. Type without serifs are called sans-serif (without serifs).

serif   sans-serif

Serifs come in two basic styles: bracketed and unbracketed. Brackets are the supportive curves which connect the serif to the stroke. Bracketed serifs curve gently into the serif from the stroke. Unbracketed serifs attach more sharply, up to a 90-degree angle.

bracketed serif   unbracketed serif

STROKE, STRESS, FLOURISH, & LIGATURE

The stroke is general name for the line (straight or curved) used in the letter, while the stress refers to the direction of thickening in a curved stroke which can give letters a slanted appearance. A swash is a flourish used to replace a terminal or serif, often extending out of the boundaries of the letter over empty space or other letters. Similarly, a ligature is a stroke joining two usually distinct letters, combining them into a single character.

DESCENDER & ASCENDER

The descender is the part of a character (g, j, p, q, y, and sometimes J) that descends below the baseline. The ascender is the part of a lowercase character (b, d, f, h, k, l, t, etc...) that extends above the mean line for the font.

PARTS

Arm/leg: Upper or lower (horizontal or diagonal) stroke that is attached on one end and free on the other.

Bar/crossbar: The horizontal stroke in characters such as A, H, R, e, and f.

Bowl: Curved stroke which creates an enclosed space within a character (the space is then called a counter).

Counter: Partially or fully enclosed space within a character.

Crotch: The pointed space where an arm meets a stem: an acute crotch less is than 90 degrees, and an obtuse crotch is more than 90 degrees.

Ear: Small stroke projecting from the top of the lowercase g.

Hairline: The thinnest line of a typeface made of varying line weight.

Link: Stroke connecting the top and bottom part (bowl and loop) of a two-storey lower case g.

Loop: Lower portion of a lower case g.

Shoulder: Curved stroke of the h, m, and n.

Spine: Main curved stroke of an S.

Spur: The small projection off a main stroke found on many capital Gs.

Stem: A straight vertical stroke or the main straight diagonal stroke in a letter which has no verticals.

Tail: Descender of a Q or short diagonal stroke of an R.

Terminal: End of a stroke not terminated with a serif.

F _{arm}

A _{bar}

B _{bowl}

e _{counter}

V _{crotch}

N _{hairline}

n _{shoulder}

S _{spine}

G _{spur}

T _{stem}

a _{terminal}

Q _{tail}

g ear link loop

TYPEFACE VARIATIONS

The standard version of the font is called the regular (sometimes normal, plain, book or roman). Variations on the standard font come in four main categories.

WEIGHT

Common weights include ultra light, extra light, light, regular, medium, demi (or semi) bold, bold, extra bold, black and ultra black. Some designers developed their own numbering systems to indicate weight. The lower the number the lighter the weight; therefore as the number increases so does the weight.

SLOPE

This category has two common names, one is italic and the other oblique. Traditionally, the italic version of a typeface is a custom drawn design based on the vertical version but with more of a calligraphic flair. Curves, stems, bowls and other characteristics are custom drawn to visually correct for the angle change and to create a difference between the vertical version and the italic. The oblique version, on the other hand is the vertical design with an angle applied to each character. It is always recommended if possible, to use a font that has either an italic or oblique version created by the designer.

When you apply an italic style by using a tag or an applied style in an HTML editor, the auto-generated italic tends to distort each character. You will end up with cleaner and more legible text in your layout by using fonts with an italic or oblique version.

WIDTH

This subset of a family includes such variations as condensed, narrow, wide, extended, and regular. These terms speak for themselves. The biggest consideration is how much turf each character takes up on the page. Short headlines in a black extended face may look great but when applied to a wordier one, the line length may become unacceptable. You will see these variations heavily used in newspaper design. The condensed version allows for a wordier headline, but comes with its own tradeoff, readability, which suffers from the reduced negative space in the characters.

SMALL CAPS

As with italics and obliques, small Caps can be generated by applications and code, but they're not the real deal. Many OpenType fonts come with small caps included and some other fonts come with an additional small cap file, some for free, others for purchase. A true small cap has the stroke width modified to match the larger character, while a computer-generated version has the character reduced, leaving the smaller character with a lighter weight.

Sans Se[rif]

ASSERTIVE AND FAMILIAR—ENFORCING ST[R...]

Gotham Book
ABCDEFGHIJKLMNOPQRS[...]
abcdefghijklmnopqrst[...]
1234567890[...]

DI.SPLAY

DISTINCT BUT UNIFIED—EACH CONTAINING A SEPARATE PERSONALITY AND POWER

LINOTYPE FRANOSCH PRO MEDIUM
ABCDEFGHIZKLMNOPQRSTUVWXYZ
ABCDEFGHIZKLMNOPQRSTUVWXYZ
1234567XYZ17

TYPES OF TYPE: DISPLAY OR BODY

Text can be used for a wide variety of purposes in a design, but we can break these down into two basic categories, which will help us later when we decide what fonts to use in our design. Historically, many typeface families would often include both body and display versions as separate fonts, each customized to the intended size. We'll discuss body and display type in more detail when we start choosing fonts in chapter 4.

DISPLAY

Display type fonts—also called titling type—are used for headlines, labels, and navigation, where emphasis is most important. These fonts are generally used at larger size and are heavier in weight than body type. These fonts will give your designs the majority of their voice.

BODY

Body type fonts—also referred to as text type or paragraph type—are used for paragraphs of text where readability is most important. These fonts are generally used at smaller sizes, so clarity is of importance.

CLASSIFYING TYPE FOR THE WEB

We based my sub-categories on the widely accepted Vox-ATypI classification system (or Vox system) with a few modifications where it made more sense for Web design.

There is a power in the ability to name things, and that's no different with type. Although it will not make you a better designer, being able to call different type styles by their recognized names will always help you describe and choose the right typeface for the job. There are actually several different methods for classifying typefaces, but the one that matters in Web design is the use of generic font family names: serif, sans-serif, cursive, fantasy, and monospace. Although the W3C system is terse, it is how we actually refer to the fonts in our CSS code.

For descriptive purposes, however, these five classifications leave a lot out. To help better understand the many different styles, we sub-divided each of those basic classifications into fifteen distinct sub-styles. It is important to note that although these sub-divisions are useful for describing fonts, they are never used in code.

SERIF

Serif fonts, as contrasted with sans serif fonts, include embellishments at the ends of a letter form that strokes. Originally intended to resemble the pen strokes of scripted type, they are now used to help spacing and differentiate the glyphs, especially at smaller sizes in print. Whether this works to improve readability is up for considerable debate, especially on screens where resolution is considerably lower than in print, but serif fonts can certainly add to the voice of the typeface.

In print, serifs improve legibility by adding by adding more visual contrast between glyphs. However, on most screens—especially at smaller sizes (12 px or below)—serifs tend to blur the letter in lower resolution monitors, making letters less distinct and less legible.

OLD STYLE

Old style typefaces are the oldest of the serif font typefaces, dating back to the mid–1400s, soon after the invention of the printing press. Their differentiating characteristic from other serif fonts is the angled stress of the letters, most noticeable in the lower case "e". Goudy Bookletter 1911 is an old style font.

TRANSITIONAL

Transitional serif typefaces are the most common serifs in use today, with Times New Roman, Baskerville, and Georgia counted in their ranks. The contrast between thick and thin strokes is stronger than in old style, and transitional styles lack the pronounced slant of old style fonts. Baskerville is a transitional serif font.

MODERN

Modern typefaces—also called Neoclassical or Di-done—have an extremely pronounced contrast between thick and thin strokes, a completely vertical stress ,and minimal brackets in their serifs (transition into serif). It is also common for these fonts to use ball-shaped serifs at their terminals for added distinction. Didot is a modern serif font.

Regain

SLAB

Slab—also called Egyptian or mechanistic serif—typefaces have almost no contrast in stroke widths with often heavy rectangular serifs with minimal or no bracketing. These fonts have become especially popular in Web design, especially for headlines, navigation and other text where clarity is important. Arvo is a slab serif font.

Regain

GLYPHIC

Glyphic typefaces have minimal triangular -shaped serifs, to the point that they are easily confused with humanist sans serif type but could also arguably be classified as serif fonts given their slightly calligraphic nature. Albertus Medium is a glyphic serif font.

Regain

SANS SERIF

Sans serif typefaces lack the flourishes of serifed typefaces and are generally clearer in appearance, although less distinctive in voice.

GROTESQUE

Grotesque sans serif typefaces have very little stroke weight contrast as compared to other serif and sans serif fonts. Grotesque fonts include some of the most common typefaces in use: Arial, Helvetica, and Gotham. News Gothic is a grotesque sans serif font.

Regain

HUMANISTIC

Humanistic sans serif typefaces have greater stroke variation than the grotesque, and many designers find them to be the most readable fonts. Gill Sans is a humanist sans serif font.

GEOMETRIC

Geometric typefaces use more basic shapes and angles in their designs. For example, the bowls of letters are generally more perfect circles or squared on a side. Geometric typefaces are less useful for body copy, but often used for titles and introductory text. Exo is a geometric sans serif font.

Regain

CURSIVE

Most type systems would not include cursive as a major category, instead calling cursive letters script or calligraphic fonts. So, while cursive type implies a more formal handwritten font, we include the more calligraphic script style and more informal handwriting style.

SCRIPT

Script typefaces—also called calligraphy—mimic calligraphic writing, like one might see on an invitation. England Hand DB is a cursive script font.

GRAPHIC

Graphic typefaces—also called brush script—are less formal handwritten styles than script, but still retain a brush or cursive-like quality. Think of hand-painted signs at a grocery store or in a garage. Knewave is a graphic cursive font.

CLASSIC SCRIPT

Classic script typefaces attempt to mimic the design of older calligraphic fonts, including Blackletter and Gaelic styles. Plain black is a cursive classic script.

HANDWRITING

Handwriting—also called casual script—typefaces mimic human handwriting, either as cursive, block letters, or a combination. Daniel is a cursive handwriting font.

WHAT ABOUT SYMBOL FONTS?

Unlike alphabetic fonts, symbol fonts—also called dingbat fonts—do not contain alphabetic characters, numbers, and other typographic symbols. Instead, the fonts contain pictograms in their place. In other words, you wouldn't use symbol fonts to lay out headlines and text, but instead you would use them in place of icons or to display simple diagrams and figures.

CSS does not contain a generic font family for symbol fonts, and these fonts have not been heavily utilized in Web design until recently, where they are beginning to take on an increasing role for creating icons in Web pages (see chapter 6).

FANTASY

Fantasy is a catch-all category for typefaces that do no readily fit into any other category. Generally, these fonts are extremely expressive, but usually only for display and unlikely to be useful for body text.

DECORATIVE

Decorative typefaces—also called ornamental—constitute the most diverse and expressive category, where fonts are specially designed to have a strong visual voice. They are generally best used as display fonts, and really work for body copy. Burnstown Dam is a decorative fantasy font.

RETRO

Retro typefaces are fonts meant to evoke the voice of a particular period, especially from the last few hundred years. Retro fonts are generally based on specific type styles from a specific period. Airstream is a retro fantasy font.

MONOSPACE

A monospace font could really come from any of the other categories, but is distinguished by spacing rather than by style. Every monospace character occupies exactly the same width as other characters in the same font, either in the character or in additional white space, allowing for consistency in spacing regardless of the exact glyphs used.

TYPE STYLES

In addition to the type classifications, there are also a number of distinct styles that are commonly applied to typefaces of all different classifications. These styles might arguably push the fonts in question into the category of fantasy, but we find it more useful when designing to use the classification system above and then use these as adjectives to help further refine the font description.

DISTRESSED

Distressed style—also called rough, textured, or grunge style—looks as if it has been weathered, eroded, crumpled up, torn, smudged, overly copied, or in some other way physically stressed or aged. Originally, this style developed when designers would literally perform those physical actions on the text to add texture or simply as a result of the duplication process, but over time, many fonts have been developed to mimic that look.

HANDDRAWN

Although often confused with the cursive handwriting class, handdrawn style fonts are meant to resemble serif, sans serif, fantasy, script or monospace fonts that have been reproduced by tracing their outline by hand. This generally means the lines are slightly wavy and may simply be the outline of the character with negative space or shading within.

STENCIL

Stencil fonts resemble text that has been created using a physical letter stencil, similar to letters often spray painted on boxes. Although typically combined with the distressed effect, you can have stencil fonts that are not distressed and distressed fonts that are not stenciled.

Regain

TYPEWRITER

Typewriter fonts resemble text output from a typewriter or daisy wheel printer. While these fonts are often monospaced, that is not a requirement. These fonts are also often combined with a distressed effect to make them look as if they were banged out on an old manual typewriter.

Regain

PIXEL

Pixel fonts resemble bitmap text that has been enlarged, such that the individual pixels become obvious. This is especially popular for games or where a low-tech voice is desired.

REGAIN

SHADED/3D

Shaded fonts include a three-dimensional (3D) shadow either behind or inside the character. Often, this might involve multiple shadows or even negative space between letter form and shadow.

REGAIN

OUTLINED

The font consists of only the outline or a pronounced gap between the outline and the interior fill.

REGAIN

ROUNDED

All or most corners in the characters are rounded off, such that there are few, if any, hard angles.

Regain

SQUARED

All or most curves in the font have been converted to angles.

REGAIN

CHARACTER AND TEXT ENCODING ON THE WEB

To a computer, a character is nothing more than a bit of code that it recognizes in order to display a particular glyph on a screen (or printer, or other output media). The shapes of letters, numbers, and other symbols are meaningless to the computer; it only knows the code to display a particular glyph that humans can understand.

Character encoding or font encoding is a system that pairs each character in a given font with the computer code used to display the glyph. With text encoding, all of the text in any document is coded by the computer, each letter having a unique code "number."

There are a number of different methods and standards that might be used to encode a font file and a text document. Imagine a computer trying to understand a different human language; if a computer doesn't understand a particular encoding "language"—or know which encoding system is being used—the text is likely to appear as gibberish.

As long as the computer program in which you are viewing the text understands the encoding used by the font and the encoding used by the text document (and all the glyphs needed to display it are included in the font, then the text will display just the way you wrote it. Even if the font and text file are encoded differently, the program will translate them. The Web has begun to standardize around a common encoding language called Unicode, which, if you stick to it, means you are unlikely to have problems with garbled text.

KNOW YOUR ENCODING: UNICODE V. ISO LATIN-1

There are literally hundreds of different character encoding systems that have been developed over the years, most famously ASCII (American Standard Code for Information Interchange), MacOS Roman (used in older versions of the Mac operating system), and multiple Windows encoding systems for different languages. Most are defined as either Western or non-Western, depending on the glyphs needed to display particular languages.

```
<meta http-equiv="Content-Type" content="text/html;
    charset=utf-8">
```

For the Web, the most common encoding system is the Unicode

```
<meta http-equiv="Content-Tye" content="text/html;
    charset=iso-8859-1">
```

format. Unicode is considered superior to other encoding methods because its entire repertoire includes over 100,000 characters from a variety of languages. A font using Unicode can contain a complete character set for multiple languages in a single font file, although that is unlikely. Fonts for specific languages tend to give results that are more acceptable to native speakers than fonts that try to cover many languages and scripts.

The most common Unicode format in use today is UTF-8. The 8 refers to how many bits are used to store each letter, meaning that a UTF-8 encoded file can contain a maximum of 256 individual characters in a single font file.

An older alternative for western language encoding that you might still run into on the Web is ISO 8859-1 (or ISO Latin 1). Similar to UTF-8, it also uses 8 bits to store characters.

Most text editors and Web editing software allow you to switch your file encoding, but our advice is to set them to UTF-8 and then walk away.

SETTING A WEB PAGE'S ENCODING

Although there are a wide variety of ways to encode a text file— HTML, CSS, a JavaScript files are all text files—encoding is rarely an issue on the Web since most browsers will automatically recognize the file's encoding type and adjust accordingly. For the most part, character encoding happens automatically and you will not need to change settings.

That said, one place you will always need to specify the encoding to be used is directly in the HTML of your document. To make sure the browser knows which encoding system you are using, in the head of your HTML, add the following line of code if you are using UTF-8: add <meta charset="UTF-8" />

If you are using ISO Latin 1, then the code is: <meta charset="iso-8859-1">

If you are using another encoding system, then you will need to replace the charset value with the appropriate encoding value. As long as the charset is defined, the browser will be able to associate the right character with the right glyph in your chosen font.

OPENTYPE

OpenType is a cross platform format that works on Windows 2000, XP and later (older versions of Windows may require ATM) versions. Apple's OS X has native support. The optimized outline structure of each glyph keeps the file sizes small, but with robust support for advanced features such as small caps, ligatures, swashed and alternate glyphs.

Many type houses are now offering Web fonts, but fonts.com has a technology that lets you unleash the power of OpenType in its OpenType enabled Web fonts. This tool allows you to use such advanced features as ligatures, small caps, fractions, alternate characters, and modify kerning pairs.

With all of these advanced features, your layout can now include smart quotes, block quotes and a wide array of typographic accents that can give your layout a clean, crisp ,and advanced look.

OpenType was launched by Microsoft in 1996 with assistance from Adobe, and the format was the next generation of Microsoft's TrueType technology. OpenType offers greater language support than its predecessor. This format has the capacity to accommodate up to 65,536 glyphs, making it ideal for international scripts.

The expanded number of glyphs also allows for additional ligatures, giving your text a customized look.

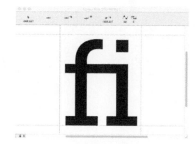

C D E F G H I J K L M N O P Q R S T U V W

Y Z [\ ] ^ _ ` a b c d e f g h i j k l m

o p q r s t u v w x y z { | } ~ € , ƒ

… † ‡ ˆ ‰ Š ‹ Œ ' ' " " • – — ˜ ™

› œ Ÿ ¡ ¢ £ ¥ ∫ © ª « ¬ – ®

± ² ³ ´ µ ¶ · , ¹ º » ¼ ½ ¾ ¿ À Á Â Ã Ä Å

Ç È É Ê Ë Ì Í Î Ï Ð Ñ Ò Ó Ô Õ Ö × Ø Ù Ú Û

Ý Þ ß à á â ã ä å æ ç è é ê ë ì í î ï ð ñ

ó ô õ ö ÷ ø ù ú û ü ý þ ÿ ⊠ ⁴ / ˚ ı Ā ā Ă

ă Ą ą Ć ć Ĉ ĉ Ċ ċ Č č Ď ď Đ đ Ē ē Ě

Ė ė Ę ę Ě ě Ĝ ĝ Ğ ğ Ġ ġ Ģ ģ Ĥ ĥ Ħ ħ Ĩ ĩ Ī

Ĭ ĭ Į į İ IJ ij Ĵ ĵ Ķ ķ ĸ Ĺ ĺ Ļ ļ Ľ ľ Ŀ ŀ Ł

Ń ń Ņ ņ Ň ň ŉ Ŋ ŋ Ō ō Ŏ ŏ Ő ˝ ő Ŕ ŕ Ŗ ŗ Ř

Ś ś Ŝ ŝ Ş ş Ţ ţ Ť ť Ŧ ł Ũ ũ Ū ū Ŭ ŭ Ů ů Ű

SCRIPT

MONOSPACE

HUMANIST

RETRO

grotesque

X CAP HEIGHT

GEOMETRIC

FIXED WIDTH

BASE

FINDING FONTS

3

Nothing exists until or unless it is observed. An artist is making something exist by observing it. And his hope for other people is that they will also make it exist by observing it. I call it 'creative observation.' Creative viewing.

William S. Burroughs

Typography is about more than typefaces and fonts, but trying to create compelling typographic design with only a single typeface available to you is like trying to paint with only one color. And if everyone only uses that one color, the world is a very monotonous place. Literally.

For the majority of the Web's history, though, that's what it was like, with only a few fonts to choose from. You now can find tens of thousands of fonts to use in your designs, but you have to know where to find them and how to use them. The issue then is finding the best solution for your type needs, considering not only the fonts you want to used, but also the technology to deploy them, the quality, and the cost.

Type foundries are releasing their libraries of both new and time-tested designs for Web use. There are a variety of pricing options out there ranging from free, one time license and pay by page views. You should never use any conversion tools to to generate Webfont files; always check with the foundry first, as most licenses only cover traditional desktop usage.

Font Foundry • Before the digital revolution and desktop publishing, type foundries cast their wares out of metal or carved wood. These designs were eventually digitized by outlining the letterforms and assigning each glyph to a keystroke. Modern foundries now supply the design community with OpenType fonts, which have become the standard file formats for such applications as Photoshop and Illustrator. Some foundries' and type distributors that carry their own and smaller foundries wares will be highlighted later in this book.

abcdefghijklmnopqrstuvwxyz
CLAVO

SOLUTIONS FOR FONTS ON THE WEB

Icons for fonts

There are three different solutions that you can choose from to specify the font used in your designs:

1 **Web-Safe Fonts** are pre-installed on the end-user's computer. Until Webfonts appeared, using Web-safe fonts was the most common method for adding typographic variety. However, the number of fonts was limited to at best a few dozen, and fewer than a dozen *called the Core Web Fonts* were capable of being installed across all platforms.

2 **Webfonts** are downloaded from a Web server, generally the same server as the HTML and CSS files, using the @font-face rule. This method requires that you control the original font-file, and can serve it, much like you serve an image file on the Web.

3 **Webfont Service Bureaus** are Webfonts downloaded from a thirdparty Web server directly to the end user's computer, and may use @font-face, linked CSS files, or JavaScript. As the name indicates, these are services that provide the font for use, but you never actually control the font file on your own server.

In this chapter we will be examining all three options in greater detail to help you find the best solution for your needs.

HOW TO EVALUATE THE BEST SOLUTION

The solution you choose will depend on a variety of different factors:

TYPEFACE VARIETY

Different solutions have different fonts available, with Web-safe fonts being the most limited. That said, not all fonts you may want to use are available to purchase, and different Webfont service bureaus have differnt fonts that they can provide.

Consider carefully the fonts or font type you want to use, then check to see whether a particualr solution will have what you are looking for.

SPECIFIC TYPEFACE REQUIRED

If your design requires a very specific font, then you will likely have to choose a specific solution—for example, if you need the font Gill Sans you will need to purchase it as a Webfont from fonts.com.

However, even if your style guide requires a specific font, it's still worth looking around for similar alternatives. For example, although you can currently only get Gill Sans from places that sell Monotype fonts, you could subsitute Humanist 521, which is an almost identical font.

COST

There are a lot of free, high-quality Webfonts. That said, higher quality or specific typefaces come at a cost. On top of that, if you want or have to use a Webfont service bureau, there will be cost involved. You will want to do some cost comparison.

Gill Sans on fonts. com

Font-squirrel's sub-setting tool

One way to increase download speed is by decreasing the number of glyphs in an individual font file. The process—called subsetting—allows you to specify the charchters you need for your designs, removing the rest.

This is especially useful for headline fonts, which may not need all of the various glyphs provided for various languages, for mathematic notation, or special typographic marks that are rarely used.

Hosting your own fonts takes some knowledge of how the Web works. If you are not fond of wrangling your own font files, managing server loads and the like, then you will probably go for a Webfont service bureau and leave the driving to them.

ADDING FONTS: THE FONT STACK

Regardless of which option you end up choosing, they all rely on creating a *font stack* using the CSS font or font-family properties. The stack is a comma-separated list of typeface names that might display your design.

STARS, UNDERSTUDIES, AND GENERICS

The first typeface selected is your preferred choice or *star* choice. The subsequent typefaces listed are are fallback—*understudy*— fonts that can perform if the star is not available.

The final font in the list should always be the *generic font family*, so that if none of the fonts in the stack is available, the computer will try to match the style as closely as it can from the fonts available on the end user's machine. For example, if you are using the font Arial, the generic font family is sans-serif. If Arial is not available, then another sans-serif font is used.

As discussed in chapter 2, there are a number of systems that can be employed to classify fonts, but the one that is most relevant to Web typography was created by the W3C to classify font families for use in CSS.

» **serif**: Times, Georgia, Garamond, Perpetua, and Rockwell.

» **sans-serif**: Helvetica, Arial, Century Gothic, and Lucida Sans.

» **monospace**: Courier, Courier New, and Andale Mono.

» **cursive**: Snell Roundhand, Bradley Hand ITC TT, Brush Script MT, and Lucida Calligraphy.

» **fantasy**: Cracked, Curlz MT, and Bauhaus 93.

FFFFALLBACK

A type diff tool that visually contrasts the differences between two fonts currently supports fonts from the Google Web Fonts library and any system fonts. Best if viewed on the latest versions of modern browsers.

CREATING A FONT STACK

Fonts are specified in Web pages as a font stack in either the font or font-family CSS property. A font stack is simply a list of typefaces that can be used in the design, with the first being the preferred font to be used—the star—followed by other typefaces to be used if the star is not available to the computer—the understudies. If the browser does not have access to the star font (Georgia, for example)—either because the font is not installed on the end user's computer or it has not been downloaded—then the next font (Times) is tried as a fall-back until all of the fonts in the list are exhausted with a generic font family type being the last resort (serif):

```
font-face: georgia, times, "times new roman", serif;
font: bold italic 1em/1.1 georgia, times, "times new roman", serif;
```

The font-family property allows you to set the typeface, while the font property is a shortcut that not only lets you set the typeface, but also the font weight (bold), font style (italic), font variant (small caps), font size, and line height all in a single line.

Sound simple? On the surface, creating a font stack is pretty straightforward; however, since you can only set the font size once, there is no way to adjust for fonts that may be larger or smaller than the star. So when choosing understudy fonts, you need to make sure they are approximately the same general width and height as the star, or you run the risk of throwing your design into dissaray.

WEB-SAFE FONTS

The makers of FontLab and Fontographer have a great tool called TransType, a universal font converter that can export Webfonts for your project. As always, please check your existing license before modifying your files.

TransType supports all major formats including .woff .eot and .svg.

Historically, Web design has been limited to the ten *core Web fonts* that most computers were guaranteed to have installed, although really only five of those were generally usable for most text. In addition to those, there are generally several dozen Web-safe fonts that will be preinstalled on the end user's computer, either by the operating system or by commonly installed software such as Microsoft Office and Apple iWork. Although you cannot guarantee that these fonts will be available, they are likely to be installed, and can be used along with the core Web fonts to create your font family font stack.

CORE WEB FONTS

Officially know as *Core fonts for the Web*, Core Web fonts are almost guaranteed to be pre-installed on all computers running the Mac and Windows operating systems. This is a list of ten type faces that both companies have licensed for their operating systems. Originally 10 fonts were selected, licensed by Microsoft and distributed widely with a number of browsers and operating systems including Windows and Mac. Andale Mono has since been removed from Windows, but is still included on the Mac.

The core fonts for the Web project ended in 2002 with Microsoft protesting that the fonts were distributed in violation

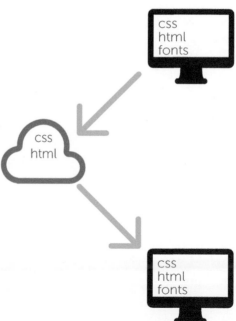

of the End User License Agreement (EULA). Still, most of the fonts from the original project are still distributed with current versions of Windows (with the exception of Andale Mono) and Mac OS X. Given that between them these operating systems make up about 96% of the market, it's a fair bet that any computer to which you send content to will have these fonts. The absence of a more reliable alternative explains why these typefaces still dominate Web typography today.

Although not inherently unsatisfactory fonts, the very fact that they are the only fonts used in Web designs has led to an inevitable backlash against their monotony. Unfortunately, there are really only five of those fonts that are useful for general design when it comes to readability for large blocks of text.

```
font-family: arial, serif;
```

OS FONTS

The OS (operating system) manufacturer will generally preinstall a few dozen or even a few hundred fonts. They vary between Mac OS, Windows, and Unix, with a little overlap, but they can also vary from OS version to OS version with some fonts added and others dropped.

For responsive design, it is also important to consider fonts installed on mobile devices as Web-safe fonts. These lists are a little

easier to predict, though, since generally fonts can only be preinstalled by the manufacturer and cannot be easily removed.

```
font-family: helvetica, arial, sans-serif;
```

SOFTWARE FONTS

Software packages are common, most especially those with image editing and word-processor applications like Microsoft Office,
Apple iWork, or Adobe Creative Suite. It is important to note that
Adobe products, while commonly installed by most designers, will
still be extremely rare for the general population.

```
font-faily: avenir, 'helvetica neue', helvetica, arial, serif;
```

WEBFONTS

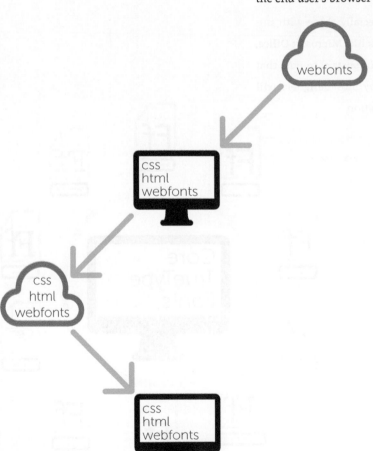

A Webfont is a font file downloaded from a Web server and used by the end user's browser to render HTML text. To use a Webfont, you begin by uploading the font file from your computer to your Web server—the same as you would upload any data file, like an image file—which in turn is downloaded to the end user's computer.

UPLOADING FONTS TO A WEB SERVER

If you've ever uploaded a file to a Web server, the process for uploading fonts to your Web server is virtually identical. Using your favorite FTP (File Transfer Protocol) application, add the font file to the directory of your choice, and use standard URL pathing to reference it in your CSS using the @font-face rule.

Although you can place the file in any directory, we recommend creating a unique fonts folder to store all fonts, similar to the way you might have CSS, javascript, or images folders for each of those file types.

LINKING FONTS

Once uploaded to the server, the font file is accessed by your Web page using the @font-face rule. This defines the source of the font file, what you want to call this font in your code, and whether the font is used for normal, bold, and/or italic and oblique styles.

The syntax for requesting a font file from a Web server is straightforward, requiring that you simply supply:

1 **Font family name**: A name to use for the font in the document. You determine what this name is, but you will need to keep it consistent throughout your code.

2 **Source**: The URL where to find the font file, either relative or absolute.

3 **Local source (optional):** The font name to be used if available on the end user's computer.

4 **Font format (*optional*)**: The font file format—Opentype or TrueType. Currently, Internet Explorer does not support this value, but we'll see later how we can make this work to our advantage.

5 **Weight, style, or stretch (*optional*)**: Define the weight, style, or variant with whcih the linked font is associated.

Most simply stated, the format looks like this:

```
@font-face {
  font-family: 'my font';
  src: url('../font/myfont.otf') format('opentype');
}
```

This will allow the Web page to access the file called caviardreams.otf which is located in the fonts folder. This example uses a relative path, but you can use absolute paths as well. We defined this font to normal style (not bold and/or italic). We can also include separate @font-face rules for bold, italic, and bold italic versions of the font. More on that in a bit.

You can now add the newly named font family to your font stack:

```
font-family: 'caviar dreams',  avenir, 'helvetica neue', helvetica,
    arial, serif;
```

Notice that we use the name of the font to name the font family caviar dreams. This may seem like the logical thing to do, but we recommend not doing this as a rule. Instead, give the font a generic name that describes what it will be used for in the design, like body copy or headers. That way, if you need to change the font used—for example because your client changes their mind 2 days before launch—you only have to change the @font-face source rather than searching through potentially thousands of lines of CSS code.

When the browser loads the Web page with this code, it will also load the font file and use its data to display the text on the page.

However, there's one snag. As mentioned previously, different browsers use different font file formats for not only computers but browsers in mobile devices as well. There are 5 basic formats supported, listed in chapter 2.

To accommodate different browsers and versions, you'll need to construct your @font-face rule so that it will provide the right format for each browser:

```
@font-face {
  font-family: 'my font';
  src:  url('../font/myfont.eot');
  src:  url('../font/myfont.eot?#iefix') format('embedded-opentype'),
        url('../font/myfont.woff') format('woff'),
        url('../font/myfont.ttf')  format('truetype');
}
```

This provides EOT, WOFF, and OTF/TTF versions of the font files, which will cover the overwhelming majority of browsers, ensuring that they all will display selected text using the same font. We left out an SVG version. Most browsers support other formats, and SVG can cause older iOS versions of Safari to crash, so let's avoid that one.

Notice that there are two sources for EOT. The first supplies the src file for IE9, while the second will be used by older versions of IE. The rule has to be structured this way, including the "?#iefx" so that IE will not choke on multiple sources.

You can now add multiple @font-face rules for each of the different styles by referencing the different font files for each:

BOLD, ITALIC, BOLD ITALIC, AND STRETCH

```
@font-face {
  font-family: 'my font';
  src:  url('../fonts/myfont_bold.eot?#iefix') format('embedded-
     opentype'),
        url('../fonts/myfont_bold.woff') format('woff'),
        url('../fonts/myfont_bold.ttf')  format('truetype');
  font-weight: bold;
  font-style: normal;
  font-stretch: normal; }
```

NAMING YOUR WEBFONTS

The obvious name to give a font is the original name of the font being loaded. However, you can call it just about anything—header, font012, bob, or jabberwocky. Currently, the common practice is to use the name of the font being downloaded as the font family name. This makes a certain amount of sense, as it identifies which font is in use.

In practice, though, your typography can change for a variety of reasons during development and later. As with CSS class or ID names, we recommend naming font families based on their function rather than what they look like. This allows you to change the font used in your Web pages by simply altering the file source rather than having to perform a find and replace throughout your code. Here are some ideas for naming your font families:

• Based on copy placement: You may want to use more recognizable terms like header, body copy, or asides.

• Based on purpose: If you will be using different fonts for similar purpose, number or add a letter identification such as header01, header 02, header 03, etc.

• Based on use in Website: If your typeface is specific to an organization or company, add that to the name. For example, ourfreelance company is called Bright Eye Media, so we might call a font family that serves as part of our corporate ID Invisible Jet Studios, or just Header.

TROUBLESHOOTING LINKED FONTS

Now you know how to get fonts downloaded and used in your Web designs, but that's the easy part. Although there are 150,00 fonts out there, you can't use them all, not for technical reasons, but for legal reasons. Every font is controlled by an End User License Agreement (EULA) which specifies what you can (and cannot) legally do with it. If you are having trouble linking to fonts after they are uploaded, here are a few troubleshooting tricks:

1 **Formats**: Do you have the correct format for the browser you are in which you want to display your account? If not, you will see the understudy fonts.

2 **Path**: Carefully check your path to ensure that it is a true match to where the file is located online. If you are using a relative path, try changing it to the absolute path.

3 **Cross-Domain**: Some font formats, font services and browsers will require that the location of the font be the same as the location of the HTML file requesting it, preventing the file from being called from Web pages in other domains.

This is a variant on the Fontspring Bulletproof @font-face syntax, which you can read more about at:

fontspring.com/blog/the-new-bulletproof-font-face-syntax

4 **Server**: You may need to check to make sure that your server has the appropriate MIME types defined for fonts. When first experimenting with downloadable fonts, this appeared to be a problem; it seems to have all but disappeared, leading us to believe that the TTF, OTF, and EOT formats were added in subsequent updates. If you encounter a problem where your fonts don't seem to download, check with your systems administrator.

FIREFOX AND THE CROSS-DOMAIN CONUNDRUM

One important warning: Firefox will not allow you to load a font from a domain other than the one on which the summoning Web page appears. That is, if your HTML file is in one domain (www.thisdomain.com) and your font file is on another domain (www.thatdomain.com), Firefox will refuse to use it unless you specifically configure your server to allow this, using *https://developer.mozilla.org/En/HTTP_access_control* HTTP Access Controls.

INSTALLING WEBFONTS ON YOUR COMPUTER

Although you do not have to install fonts directly on your computer for them to work as Webfonts, it is often helpful to have them handy. The problem is that once a font is installed on your local computer, the browser will default to using that font with your font stack.

END USER LICENSE AGREEMENTS AND YOU

Our best estimate is that there are somewhere around 150,000 digital fonts available to choose from, at least for print design. In theory—as long as you can convert them to the right file formats—then you can use any of these in your Web designs. However, in reality there are actually only about 40,000 that you can currently use legally in your Web designs. "Legally" is the important word here, because not all fonts are licensed to be used on the Web.

An End User License Agreement (EULA) is the agreement you make on what you can legally do (and not do) with a particular piece of software, which, in this case, is a font file. While it would be easy to think that this is just a formality, most fonts do not explicitly allow you to download them for use on a Web page with the @font-face rule. Unless it's explicitly stated, it is implicitly illegal to do so. Put another way, if your font file is not licensed for Webfont use, you are breaking the law if you use it that way. Some will argue that this is similar to downloading music or movies for free, but that's illegal too. It doesn't matter how easy it is to download, you are still breaking the law.

I'll leave it up to your conscience as to whether you think this is acceptable, but keep in mind that type makers can spend months or sometimes years developing a really good font. These fonts constitute their intellectual property (IP), and the type makers deserve to be rewarded for their hard work.

BUYING WEBFONTS AND FREE WEBFONTS

The obvious advantage of buying fonts is that you pay for the files once, and the files are yours to use on as many Websites you want and for as many visitors as your site can stand. Well almost. When you buy fonts or download them for free, the font file is yours and you can deploy it however you see fit within the confines of the EULA. This is not unlike buying a DVD. Most of us think of the DVD as our property, to do with as we please. However, if you read the fine print in the license more carefully, there are generally many things you cannot do with the video, such as show it to groups over a certain size, or copy and resell it. Font licenses may have similar restrictions.

Make sure to check the font info (shown here in the Apple Font Book) to get the license details. This one for the typeface Fanwood Text not only gives a detailed license, it also provides other useful information, like the number of glyphs included.]

Most fonts you buy or download for free, can have very few restrictions—other than not reselling them or letting other people use them without buying their own license. Especially helpful is that you can use them in Photoshop or Fireworks to create your visual comps after you install them on your computer, although most may charge a bit more for both Webfont and desktop licenses.

When purchasing fonts for Web usage, look for sites that clearly mark whether a font is licensed to be used with @font-face

Font Book's Information Panel

or not. Many use a clear label or icon, but sometimes you will need to verify their licensing plans. Hopefully that will change.

The following fonts are free or available for purchase

FREE WEBFONTS

FONT SQUIRREL

GOOGLE WEBFONTS

PURCHASE WEBFONTS

FONTSPRING

FONTS.COM

INDEPENDENT TYPE FOUNDRIES

CONVERTING TO WEBFONT

You can take an existing font file that you own or created and use FontSquirrel's @font-face generator to convert one file to all of the different formats you need to ensure full cross browser support.

The first question you need to ask before even thinking about converting an existing font file to use as a Web font is "Can I do

this legally?" To reiterate: if you can't find it explicitly stated in the license that came along with the font that it's legal to convert, then it is not. If in doubt, you can check with the license owner, generally included with information about the font in a program like Apple's FontBook.

After that, the actual font conversion is relatively easy. Although there are a variety of tools for converting fonts between formats, without doubt the easiest and most versatile is the @font-face Generator provided at FontSquirrel (http://www.fontsquirrel.com/fontface/generator).

The FontSquirrel @font-face Generator is a website that allows you to upload TTF or OTF files and, choose from a number of customization options, including:

» **Basic**: Converts the font files with no frills.

» **Optimal**: Applies certain optimization features to improve the quality and speed of the font.

» **Expert**: Gives you complete control of the conversion, including format, CSS code syntax, font subsetting, opentype options, and postscript hinting, to a name a few.

Regardless of which option you choose, the final box asks you to confirm that the font is "legally eligible for Web font embedding." You have to check it to continue, but any liability is on your shoulders.

The FontSquirrel @font-face Generator is constantly updated and refined, and provides excellent documentation on updates and how to use the product.

ALLOWING FIREFOX CROSS-DOMAIN WEBFONTS

In our case, serving the font from the same domain as our post isn't an option (unless we jump ship from Blogger and self host our blog). But, there is a way for the Web Server to tell Firefox it's OK to use the font. We I edited the Apache configuration (/etc/apache2/apache2.conf in my case), adding the following lines: AddType application/vnd.ms-fontobject .eot AddType font/ttf .ttf AddType font/otf .otf <FilesMatch ".(ttf|otf|eot)$"> <IfModule mod_headers.c> Header set Access-Control-Allow-Origin "*" </IfModule> </FilesMatch>

The AddType directive adds the appropriate MIME types to the HTTP response. The <FilesMatch> directive applies the directives it encloses only to files with extensions .ttf, .otf, and .eot. The <IfModule> directive checks to see that the Apache header module is loaded. And finally when those conditions are met, we set the Access-Control-Allow-Origin header to *. You can also put these directives into a .htaccess file.

In our case there was one other thing we needed to do on the server. We didn't have the headers module loaded in Apache, so we added it and restarted: sudo a2enmod headers sudo /etc/init.d/apache2 restart After that, the font started rendering in Firefox, even though it came from a different domain. If you are still having problems, note that you can view the HTTP headers returned from the server using the Net panel of Firebug.

WEBFONT SERVICE BUREAUS

New Webfont retailers and WFSBs coming on line all the time, and some will not will not succeed. Your primary concern is to find one that provides the proper formats to support all of the browsers and has the typefaces that best meet your design needs. You will need EOT, WOFF, and either TTF or OTF formats for the widest support. Some services will also include the SVG format, but, as explained earlier, we don't recommend using this format.

With WFSBs, you give up direct control over a file. This can have its advantages as well, since you don't have to worry about updates, cross domain issues, and you know that the font files are legal. It can also reduce the strain on your server, since you are no longer the system delivering the files. Some WFSBs use the @font-face rule for adding fonts, but more often you will be indirectly referencing the file through a linked CSS file or even using JavaScript.

WHAT TO LOOK FOR

The solution you choose will need to meet your design needs. For example, when considering using a WFSB, if your styleguide requires the use of a specific typeface, the requirement can severely limit your choice of services. This may require some shopping around, but we recommend being open to choosing other fonts for your Web site and widening your style guide accordingly.

Beyond those criteria, consider these questions when you are evaluating a potential font supplier.

» How many Webfonts are available? You should always make sure that the fonts include the ability for use with the @font-face rule. Remember, unless that is stated explicitly, the fontcan not be used legally as a Webfont.

» What code is used to embed the fonts? Web fonts are embedded using the @font-face rule; however WFSBs will often have you use a link to an external CSS file or even JavaScript to add the @font-face code.

» Can you use the font locally to create visual compositions and style guides? Many Web designs start life as visual compositions, created in an application like Photoshop or FireWorks. However, without a local version of the font, you cannot create them with Webfonts.

» Can you subset the font? One way to reduce a font file size is to eliminate glyphs that you don't need. For example, if your Website will only be displayed in English, then you can take out all of the characters not used. Some fonts will include letters for French, Spanish, German, Russian, Chinese and a multitude of other languages. omitting can radically reduce the file size, and thus increase the display speed.

» Are the fonts optimized for the screen? Most fonts were designed for print and not for screen display. Although technologies are rapidly advancing to the point that screen resolution will rival print (around 300 dpi), most people still view text on a screen with only 96 dpi. To be useful on the screen, many fonts need to be tweaked to look their best.

» Are there any limitations on amount of usage? Many services will charge rates based on bandwidth usage or page views. You will need to calculate your usage to find the best plan for your needs.

» What is the cost? Although often based on usage, cost rates vary greatly from service to service, and none use the same rates.

WFSB TECHNOLOGIES

@font-face will use code that looks almost exactly like the code used to access local Webfonts, but the URL for the font will point to the WFSB's Web server where the fonts are located.

External CSS will link to an external CSS file on another server with the @font-face code used to load the webfonts from that remote server. With linked CSS files, you lose a lot of the control you have with local files. Some systems will allow you to name the font file, but generally you are stuck with whatever name they have defined.

• **External JavaScript** will load JavaScript code, that in turn loads the fonts from the WFSB's server. The exact nature of the code is proprietary to the WFSB, but it is felt that using JavaScript adds a further level of protection to the Webfonts, preventing them from being used unlicensed use. You are stuck with whatever font name the WFSB has defined.

WFSB COST

The other vexing issue with WFSBs is that no two have the same bandwidth allowance or cost structure, making comparisons between services difficult. Obviously your criterion will be whether the WFSB has the right fonts for you. Beyond that, you want to carefully consider the following:

» Site traffic: Will your site grow or spike past the usage level you or your client are paying for? You don't want to suddenly get a big bill from the WFSB just because your site is temporarily popular.

» Long-term costs: You will be paying the fee on a regular basis, so make sure to budget for it.

» Renewal: Most services will send you a reminder when it's time to renew the license, but make sure that you have accounted for the license expiration by including understudy fonts that will replace the service if something happens.

» Client transfer: If you are purchasing for a client, you will also want to consider how easy it will be to transfer a license to your client after you purchase it.

TYPEKIT

This is Adobe's subscription-based Webfont service. It is now part of its Creative Cloud monthly subscription. This service allows you to set up font stacks in Dreamweaver and Muse.

CLOUD.TYPOGRAPHY

Hoefler & Company's Webfont subscription service, ties pricing to page views. Visit the site for current plans. Just insert their key into your CSS and start utilizing the company's fonts.

WEBTYPE

This collaboration of the Font Bureau, Roger Black and Petr VanBlokland has a wide variety of Webfonts to choose from. Subscription rates are based on traffic, and are set up on a yearly basis.

FONTS.COM

This is Monotype's Webfont presence, serving its own fonts, plus those of many additional foundries and designers. The company uses various price points, and rates are based on page views on a monthly basis.

GOOGLE WEBFONTS

This is a free service offering a wide variety of typefaces.

YOU WORK FOR THEM

This company started selling Webfonts in 2011 based on the more familiar desktop model. It charges a one-time fee, but if your site's popularity grows beyond your license, upgrades are available.

CREATING OR BUYING A CUSTOM FONT

Although there are tens of thousands of professionally designed typefaces available, you may want to create your own from scratch, especially if you want a unique handwriting style font. There are several applications, for a variety of skill levels, that make creating fonts relatively easy. iFontMake for the iPad allows you to draw glyphs for all ASCII charachters, adjust them, and then output them in a variety of formats.

Beyond making your own font, though, if you are looking for a truly unique handcrafted font, many type makers are available for hire to create fonts. These can cost a few thousand dollars for a single font to tens of thousands of dollars for a full typeface range, and so are generally purchased by larger companies looking to clearly differentiate their brands through typography.

SUB-SETTiNG FONTS

Sub-setting speeds up a site's performance by only downloading the characters or glyphs that are in your copy to the user's computer. Foreign characters, for example, will more than likely be the first candidates to go. Many font services mentioned already use this practice, like Fonts.com and Typekit. Just tweak some of their admin settings and you're good to go. FontDeck even has customized subsets with special numerals and swashes.

If you are self hosting you fonts, subsetting becomes a bit more complex.

Fontforge allows you to cut unnecessary characters from your set, the process is well documented on their site.

Font Squirrel also has an online webfont generator that exports a customized sub-set.

CHOOSE FONTS

4

From everyone to whom much has been given, much will be required

Luke 12:48 (Amplified Bible)

Henry Ford is renowned for saying, "Any customer can have a car painted any color that he [sic] wants so long as it is black." It's a relief, in a way, not to have the burden of choice. It frees us from making the wrong choice, but at the some time, it limits freedom of expression. Choices can be scary, but never fear: there is some method to the madness of choosing the right typeface for your project.

I have spent hours looking for the right typeface to use in a Web design project. It may seem simple, and—ndeed before Webfonts it was because you only had five real choices. We now have tens of thousands of fonts at our disposal, with new ones becoming available all the time.

When choosing a font, you will want to consider a few technical aspects does the font have all of the characters and styles you need? Do you want to consider how readable and memorable it will be to your audience? To do this, you have to think about the voice you want your text to take on by the typeface you choose.

Copy • Refers to the text on a page to differentiate it from other elements on the page such as images and video. **Body copy** refers to the specific long form text on the screen, generally the main content.

Type • Refers to how text on the page is displayed. **Body type** refers to the typeface used to display body copy.

ABCDEFGHIJKLMNOPQRSTUVWXYZ
abcdefghijklmnopqrstuvwxyz
0123456789
BIRCH STD

TYPES OF TYPE

Headers can serve a dual purpose, as navigation when used in an index or on a home page.

There are two basic kinds of text referred to in a design: display and body. You can refer to these on the screen as display copy or text or body copy or text, and the fonts used for them as display type/font and body type or font.

Before deciding on the typeface(s) you will be using, it's important to understand whether will be using them for display, body, or both.

DISPLAY TYPE

Display type is text on the page that is meant to stand apart from the longer form copy, usually by contrasting it in via typeface, size, style, or color. This can include titling, navigation, controls, captions, labels, and other short form text on the page. The intent of display copy is to make it quickly scannable, to catch the viewer's attention, and be easily differentiated from the body copy.

In HTML, there are six distinct header levels to account for, but in practice, it is rare to see more than three or four used in a design.

HEADERS AND HEADLINES

Copy for titles, subtitles, section heads, article headlines, and other shorter text is used to identify the topic of the body text and will contrast with other text, most often in size, spacing, and weight by default. However color, font, and other styles can also be added.

Traditionally, display type was a specific font style, generally created for use at larger sizes for headlines. With the rise of the

For an interesting read on handwriting fonts, visit https://www.smashingmagazine.com/2014/06/hands-on-sigmund-freud-typeface-making-fonts/

Common Formatting Styles:

Header/Headline

Navigation

Byline

Article

Abstract

Blockquote

Citation

Table

List

Web, that meaning has shifted to refer to any type on the page that is decorative in nature.

Some fonts are specifically designed to be used only for display type—especially in the fantasy family—and may even have "display" as part of the font name. In such cases, these fonts generally do not work well at small sizes of ~18 px or lower.

THE HEADLINE FONT

NAVIGATION AND CONTROLS

Navigation refers to the global and sectional elements and menus in a Web page used to move around within it. This can include dynamic menus in the header or sidebars, read-more links, and even may be combined with headers as navigation to articles.

Controls will often resemble navigation and other links, but are used to control actions within a page rather than move between different pages. Controls can include form elements such as check boxes and radio buttons, but in modern Web interfaces, may include a variety of menus and other options.

Although navigation, controls, and hypertext links in the body copy all use the same basic code, it's important to think of them as separate entities. Although you may style them similarly, depending on your design needs, they are conceptually different. Navigation typically uses text, but not always. Many sites may use a combination of text and icons or icons alone. Controls can be text, icons, or a combination of both, but are increasingly more likely to be icons.

BYLINES AND DATES

There are a number of special kinds of sub-headers used to provide information on the page that falls outside the body copy. These are generally specific formats, like dates, and are often meant to be de-emphasized so as not to distract from the important content of the page.

BODY TYPE

Body type is meant to be as readable and as memorable as possible to display the main content of the page, generally longer form text of a few sentences or more.

ARTICLE

Most often, body copy refers to the main text on the page, generally an article with paragraphs, block quotes, and lists. The body copy will also include hypertext links, which should be styled differently from other navigation, controls, and links on the page, but should integrate well with the rest of the body copy.

THE "WORKHORSE" FONT

ABSTRACT

Abstracts are generally short paragraph blurbs that will accompany an article headline on the front page of a Website or blog.

BLOCKQUOTES AND CITATIONS

Blockquotes represent a special form of body copy, in which a long form quote is contrasted from the article text. In addition, the quote is generally accompanied by a citation which is also styled to contrast from the main body and the blockquotes.

TABLES

Tables are often set using the same typeface as the body, or may mix display and body typefaces for the table headers and data, respectively.

LISTS

Lists will generally use the body type and use bullets or numbers to separate each item.

CAPTIONS, LABELS AND SMALL-PRINT

There are a variety of other elements on the page that will generally use the body type, but be visually contrasted in other ways.

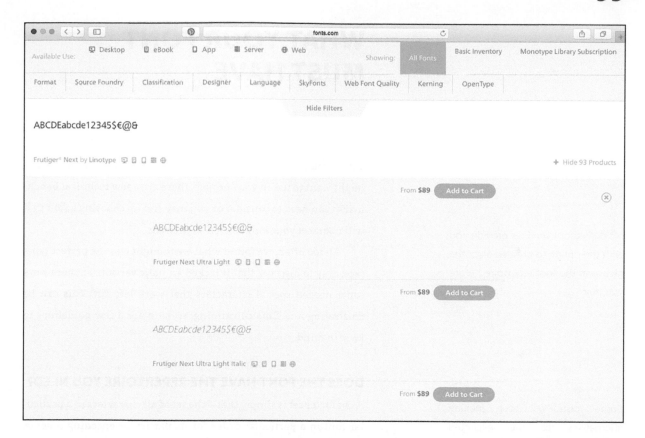

Many sites, like Fonts.com, allow designers to audition the many weights available in a Webfont, insuring a project's needs are met.

WHAT YOUR FONT MUST HAVE

Before you start looking through catalogs of possible typefaces you might want to use in your project, there are a few technical benchmarks you need to consider or you may end up choosing a font that will not meet your long-term design needs.

All too often, we found what we thought was the perfect typeface, only to discover that it lacked an italic version, or there were some needed special characters that were left out. This can be frustrating and time consuming, so here are a few guidelines to keep in mind.

Most Webfont services provide you with the option to preview all of the glyphs in the font repertoire before you buy.

DOES THE FONT HAVE THE REPERTOIRE YOU NEED?

A character set is simply that—the set of all characters in a particular font in a particular order for its particular encoding scheme, that includes less common punctuation marks. However, a font character set does not necessarily include every possible character that you may need.

If the font does not include a particular character in its repertoire, the results will be dependent on how the particular application handles nonexistent characters, but will not yield the result you want. Generally a placeholder glyph will be used, such as a rectangle with a diamond with a question mark ◊? or a rectangular box [] or just empty space.

Some fonts will even include alternatives to the expected characters. This is, in fact, how a symbol font works—each letter space contains the information used to display a pictogram glyph rather than a letter or other character.

Missing characters are rarely a problem with English language since most common fonts include a full repertoire of 26 English alphabetic characters in both upper and lower case along with common punctuation. Most professionally created fonts will include the entire "Latin" character set used to display Western languages.Generally more specialized and decorative fonts will give you problems.

CHECKING THE FONT REPERTOIRE

When designing for the Web, you must make sure that the fonts you choose contain all of the characters you need to render your text. For English, this is not usually a problem. But if you are working with content for other European languages, it is best to check the repertoire to make sure that it contains all of the umlauts, accent marks, and angle quotes needed to properly render the text.

How you check your fonts repertoire will depend on your operating system or on what software you have installed.

» **Windows**: Open the Fonts Control Panel application (which can be found through Programs > Accessories > System Tools), and choose the font from the list you want to view,

» **Mac OS**: Open the Font Book application, choose the font you want to view and then choose Preview»Repertoire (Cmd-2). You will probably need to open the typeface group to select an individual font. You will see a table showing every glyph available in the selected font.

Many display fonts only include upper case glyphs.

NON-WESTERN FONTS

Although this book primarily deals with typography in Western alphabets, there are numerous other languages that many Web designers will need to take into account, whether they speak the languages or not.

Obviously, having a knowledge of the language you are designing for is preferable, but if you don't have time for a crash course, most of the general technical and visual rules for typography will stay much the same. For example, regardless of the language you are designing for, you need to ensure that the font you select contains all of the glyphs you need to properly display that language. If in doubt, find someone who knows the language in question to help you.

» **Other ways** to check the repertoire of a particular font you have installed are to use programs like PopChar (ergonis.com/popchar) that display the entire font repertoires, and allow you to quickly choose a particular glyph.

DOES THE TYPEFACE HAVE THE WEIGHTS AND STYLES YOU NEED?

Remember that a font is a single style or weight of a particular typeface. Many typefaces consist of only a single font, with no variations. This may be acceptable for display type, but for body type you are likely going to at least need italics, bold, and possibly bold/italic to ensure the highest quality display.

You may notice, though, that even if the typeface you are using does not have an explicit bold or italic/oblique font, it will appear bold and oblique when you ask it to, but these fonts are useless. In cases where a weight or style is required that is not available in the typeface repertoire, the browser will synthesize that weight or style, tilting the regular style to make an oblique font and thickening the outline of the regular appearance to make the text bold. This is bad typography.

Weights and styles are not created by simply thickening or slanting the regular style of the font. Typemakers spend time designing these alternate versions to ensure that the individual glyphs display optimally. Browser-simulated weights and styles will be less aesthetically appealing. Although the reader may not be able to put a finger on the problem, when a proper bold or italic/oblique font is used, the subtle smoothness will contribute to the overall readability of the text.

It is important to determine the editorial styles at this point. You may decide that bold is never to be used in body copy, for example, so you don't need a bold font. You may also decide that you want to use three different weights of bold for different purposes, and thus need to make sure that the typeface you choose accommodates this need. If you are writing in English, the standard for citation choice for books, movies, and other media is italics.

Display copy gets a little bit more tricky to choose, since you are less likely to need a bolder option. However, if you plan on including book, movie, or other titles in a headline, find a typeface with an italic/oblique version. Again, look carefully at the text you plan on presenting. It may be that you pick one font for your primary headers, navigation, and controls, and a separate one for article headlines.

HAS THE FONT BEEN OPTIMIZED FOR THE SCREEN?

Some fonts are better than others for the screen. Keep in mind that before 2008, virtually all fonts were designed to be printed. There are some exceptions, but most type designers were more concerned with print than pixels. Most modern fonts have been optimized for the screen and for the Web, especially those obtained from a Webfont service bureau.

Fonts that have been specifically adjusted for screen resolutions are generally preferable to those that have been retrofitted. Known as **hinting**, screen optimized fonts have had their anti-aliasing adjusted for the screen. Remember that fonts are vector based and stored as outlines. These outlines are for print at 300+ dpi, with screen display an after thought. However, as more text is displayed solely to be read on a screen at 72 to 96 dpi, the font outlines need to be manually adjusted by the Typemakers.

Whether this has been done is not always obvious, but if your font seems to look smudged at smaller sizes, losing its crisp edges, then it's likely not been hinted for the screen.

IS THE FONT CROSS-PLATFORM COMPATIBLE?

It is important to check the font you choose for how it will display in as many of the operating system's in which it will be displayed, as you can. Many browsers render type using the operating systems rendering engine to anti-alias type. But not all OSs are created equal in that regard. Whereas the Mac consistently uses its Core-Text system, Windows systems may be using different anti-aliasing method, depending on the user preference or installed software (see chapter 2).

Because of these differences, fonts that look great on a Mac may not look nearly as good on a PC running Windows. Another advantage of Webfont service bureaus is that they have checked all these issues, and generally ensure cross-platform compatibility of any fonts they serve. However, it's always a good idea to do a quick check of how the font appears on various platforms before you commit to it.

FACTORS TO CONSIDER

The technical criteria are important to keep in mind while making your decision, but not necessarily the basis for choosing a typeface. Traditionally, type is selected against three basic criteria: legibility, readability, and voice. To that mix, it is becoming increasingly apparent that we need to consider how well the information read is retained, which, as it turns out is also a function of the typeface.

Legibility deals with how clearly recognizable the characters are from each other, while readability deals with how easy the text is to read as an aggregate. Readability and legibility are, obviously, also functions of the typography, not just the font, but you can choose fonts that will be inherently more readable and legible out of the gate.

However, the purpose of reading text is actually **not** to read it as quickly as possible, which is what legibility and readability are primarily concerned with. The purpose of text is to convey information that the reader retains. Obviously, the faster the reader can achieve that goal, the better, but rushing through information and then immediately forgetting it is a failed typographic goal. Instead, we want to choose fonts that balance legibility, readability, and voice while promoting the retention of information.

TYPE TRANSPARENCY?

Not all fonts are created to maximize legibility, especially display type where the voice of the type may need to dominate. However, high legibility is generally a good feature to look for in body copy to avoid eye strain.

In cases where legibility is important, typefaces are often intended to be "transparent," so that the reader is as unaware of the letter forms as possible. The better designs are those that do not get in the way of relating the information.

Unfortunately, it is difficult to balance the need for transparency against the danger of becoming monotonous. If your text is dull, completely, you run the risk of losing your audience's attention. In chapter 6, we'll consider how the font and styles come together to promote user understanding of what is being read.

Given the need for consistent strokes and strong serifs for legibility on the screen, it's no surprise that slab serif fonts have become so popular over the last few years.

CHOOSE FOR LEGIBILITY AND READABILITY

Legibility is the ease of the reader to grasp the individual parts of the text–the features in type that allow the individual glyphs to be quickly perceived by the viewer. This is important for ensuring that the text can be quickly read and understood. Readability is the slightly nebulous feature of type that allows it to be read over an extended period, with minimal fatigue. Although text relies on legibility, readability is also a function of the general layout as well.

While you are choosing your fonts, consider these traits to improve legibility and readability.

CONSISTENT LIGHT STROKES

Although variations in the stroke width add visual interest and variation to the type, they can also be harder to read over long stretches. Having little variation in the strokes between thick and thin tends to be more readable and thinner strokes are more legible.

NO SERIFS OR STRONG SERIFS

There is considerable debate over whether serifs improve readability or not, although there is little doubt that they add to the voice of the font .For body copy on the screen, going with no serifs (sansserif) or strongly bracketed serifs is best. This has much to do with the the way in which fonts on the screen are anti-aliased for rendering (see chapter 2), where the edges of the glyphs are "blurred" to give the illusion of sharper edges. Fine serifs in a font will tend to look blurred or smudged, giving them less definition and thus rendering them harder to read.

BALANCE COUNTER WIDTH, LETTER WIDTH, AND X-HEIGHT

In general, larger counter widths, wider letters, and a taller x-height will create more legible, readable text. Counters, the empty spaces within letters such as "o", "p", and "u" are as important for defining the character as the "painted" portions. More open space tends to exaggerate the x-heights and widths of letters. However, you can have too much of a good thing. Balance between these three properties is always preferred.

Since over 95% of the letters in text are lower case, having them larger compared to upper case text improves readability. However, this is not an absolute rule. Instead, when the ratio of the x-height is low, then the type you choose will need to be set at a larger font size, which we will look at in more detail in chapter 5.

CHOOSE FOR VOICE

Consider the simple I phrase "I'm going to kill you." On the face of it, the meaning seems straightforward, but as anyone who has ever used this phrase in everyday conversation can attest, it is rarely meant to be taken literally. Instead, the tones and inflection in the voice of the speaker reflect the true meaning. If the words are spoken in an exasperated tone of voice, they are meant to show the speaker is at his or her wit's end. If spoken in a mechanical tone, we may be facing robo-apocalypse. If spoken in soothing tone of voice, the statement might be a form of seduction, if the speaker sounds like a pirate, you probably should start considering walking the plank.

Typography gives voice to text, but in Web design much of the typography is simply left to the default values set for a particular operating system or application. Imagine if everyone spoke in the same tone of voice, never varying from one person to the next. The same inflection and cadence spoken monotonously is what we see today on the Web, not only because of the seemingly limited font family choices, but because so much is left to the defaults.

Although the type you use communicates a great deal of visual information, most people when dealing with a blank word processor page, e-mail or blog entry, tend to use whatever values the software makers have set as the default.

A widely accepted truism of the Web is that "content is king" and since much of the content on any given Web page will be text, text is the king of content. This is especially true when you consider that search engines primarily look at text and its context in order to rank pages for relevancy.

Typography should always be at the service of the text it is presenting, but to understand that type, and thus develop the most effective typographic voice for that text, you must consider:

1 What is the tone of the content?

2 Who is the audience for the content?

3 How strong or loud do you want the voice to come across?

SPECIAL FONTS FOR DYSLEXIC USERS

Dyslexia is a common reading problem, affecting around 10% of literate people—more people than suffer from red–green color blindness. But, while designers regularly consider how a lack of color perception might affect their designs, we should consider ways to help dyslexic readers.

Based on their findings, the researchers recommended Helvetica, Courier, Arial, Verdana and Computer Modern, based both on reading performance and subjective preference; and cautioned against the use of italic texts.

The Dyslexia.com and OpenDyslexic.com sites provide more information on this condition.

COMBINING TYPE

There are no hard and fast rules that say you cannot use the same typeface for both display and body type, or that you can't choose a display typeface for larger sizes and another for smaller type sizes. You will also find that you may want to pick a typeface for the display text with multiple weights and styles that you can then mix and match.

It is rare, however, that you will want to mix more than two typefaces in a single design. While not impossible, it takes a lot of skill, practice, and testing to pull that off successfully.

STRUCTURE

Is your font selection geometric, or calligraphic in nature? Combining a geometric typeface with a calligraphic may create visual tension, but more than likely will draw too much attention to the faces' differences rather than to your content. Structure can summon an era. For example, tall slender letter forms with high weight contrasts can summon the Art Deco period while tall, narrow geometric designs can echo the Russian Constructivist period.

SCALE

Is the design narrow (condensed) or is it extended? Scale in both width and height can play with positive and negative space in an elegant way. Many typefaces, especially those in the Grotesque camp are already geometric and extended. The Swiss developed an interesting design style, heavily influenced by the geometry of Helvetica. The Swiss style employs a grid structure and sometimes dramatic changes in type size to move the eye through the page.

CLASSIFICATION

Chapter 2 explained typeface classifications and how you can use these structural differences to create visual tension in your design. Serifs, stroke weights, and geometry all have their own special attributes, and can be teamed to create a compelling visual hierarchy.

These classifications can influence the look and feel in many other ways. A stark serif face with a conservative color palette can convey a legal or scholarly tone, while a few sans serif designs mixed in a judicious way can lend a corporate feel.

MOOD AND COLOR

Mood and color can set the tone for your site and speak to your demographic with a visual vernacular. A retro typeface and color palette will give your layout a warm and hospitable feel, and perhaps speak to specific audiences, or convey the spirit of a time period. A tech font with a pixelated look mixed with brighter colors will more than likely speak to video game buffs.

EXTREME CONTRAST

Extreme contrast between your display and body copy typefaces can give a visual tension . These differences may include stroke quality and weight, positive and negative space, character width, and visual density.

CHECKLIST FOR CHOOSING TYPE

» Will the font's weights, styles and variations grow with your site? As mentioned, a condensed, and extended version can give a different look and feel, without the need for an additional typeface beyond your chosen family.

» Does the typeface have an italic or oblique style? This is important for obvious reasons such as referencing books and periodicals, foreign phrases or when words imitate sounds.

» Consider reviewing every character from the font, and testing it in body copy and headlines. Sometimes you may like most all of the glyphs, but one or two characters do not fit your needs.

» How is your font licensed? Will you receive a surprise bill if your site gets a lot of traffic from a blog posting or news item?

» If your client already has a corporate font, can you legally convert it to a Webfont? Will you have to purchase additional licenses from the foundry?

INTERVIEW WITH NICOLE ARNETT PHILLIPS

Nicole Arnett Phillips is an Australia-based designer and the proprietor of the blog TypogrpHer, as well as the publisher of the Typograph.Journal. Both cover the field of typography and graphic design

Size and scale can help a viewer quickly read text. How do you determine the sizes for your various headers? Do you use a mathematical approach, intuition, or a mixture of the two?

My approach starts with the content. I look at what sort of hierarchy will be required. Is there only one level of heading or are there sub headings too. Does the text use bold words and phrases for emphasis within the text? Are there pull features and quotes? Once I have read and understood the content, I then determine my body text size and then work upward (from smallest text sizes to largest) in mathematical increments to establish the size for all the other paragraph styles. I do occasionally use intuitive or optical-based interventions to the hierarchy if the scale if something looks particularly heavy or a layout looks disproportionate.

What helps you select a typeface family for a project? Do you lean toward a wide variety of styles within the family, like Condensed, Extended, Roman and Light?

First and foremost I am guided by tone—typography is the voice of the text. I don't talk to my consulting clients in the same voice I use to toilet train my puppy. And the same is true when we communicate visually. I always aim to select a voice most appropriate to the meaning of the text; that is my first concern in typeface selection Next is construction. I find a lot of really beautifully constructed letter forms are let down by poor spacing in fonts. So if a typeface is comprised of a beautiful collection of black shapes but the white shapes and spaces are awkward and going to create a lot of work for tracking and kerning, I will discount that face in my selection process. I want the typeface to be well constructed and perform well so the typesetting is fluid and easy. As far as looking for a wide variety of styles, this would be determined by the content. If the job has a complex hierarchy and requires lots of different paragraph styles, then a variety of weights and styles becomes important to ensure you can express the meaning and structure of the content in a consistent voice. But if the text is more simple, that variety becomes less important. There are a lot of great typefaces only available in Roman, bold and italic.

Designers often use a grid to create structure, but occasionally you need to break it to successfully draw attention to content or to give design a unique feel. What advice do you have for breaking the grid?

I always start with a grid or some mathematical guidelines in my work but love to break the grid in my designs departure from an established layout convention can create impact, and grab attention when done correctly. So my main advice here is to always start with a set of visual rules and fully understand them before breaking them! This way when you do reject or subvert the grid in your composition, you are doing it with purpose to create meaning or alter the reader experience.

Color can help move the eye throughout a page, but it can also be a distraction. Clients often have existing color palettes, limiting your creativity. When you start a project from scratch, what issues and elements do you consider while selecting your palette?

I really like to use color for emphasis, so I try to select color palettes that have harmony and contrast. I want some colors to be recessive and play supporting roles in my designs and others to be the stars and really pop out. I am also a big fan of black (particularly in text andtype) so I usually start with one to three hero colors (including black) as my primary palette and then choose one or two more recessive tints and neutral shades as my secondary supporting palette. Most of my projects that use color are limited to five (or fewer) tones. For example, TypographJournal volume 03 uses black, 172U, a 70% tint of 172U and two black tints (27% and 70%). The typographer.com Website uses Black(R0, G0, B0), grey(R109, G111, B113), turquoise(R64, G191, B187), and coral(R255, G103, B76).

Connect with Nicole at:

typograph.Her

Typographic Musings for Curious Creatives

www.typographHer.com

true type flavor

OPEN
TYPE
.W

5

"I AM BASICALLY ANALYTICAL, NOT CREATIVE; MY WRITING IS SIMPLY A CREATIVE WAY OF HANDLING ANALYSIS."

PHILLIP K. DICK

The fonts are the voice you give your text, and the styles you apply add the inflection and tone to that voice. Although Web design seems to have a limited number of text styles (color, bold, italic, text case, decoration, and text shadow) combining all of these components can create a surprising number of effects.

Styles are where designers do a lot of work, and tie closely into the work you will do to create a strong hierarchy of information throughout the entire design at the macro level, which we will discuss more in chapter 8. In this chapter, we are just concerning ourselves with how to apply the basic styles to the text (the micro level).

Before you start adding styles to your text, though, it is important to make sure that you create a consistent baseline to start from. All browsers have default styles that they apply to text in the absence of any styles you define. Begin any new project by first resetting the basic styles, and then developing a style guide that you or your staff or clients can refer to while working.

ABCDEFGHIJKLMNOPQRSTUVWXYZ
FURORE

CONSISTENCY IN STYLES

One problem designers face with browsers is making sure that what they create looks the same or at least as close to the same as possible across a growing number of applications and devices. It's no longer enough just to design for a single Web browser, with the ever growing number of places your designs might be seen, you need to set some baselines and create a consistent style guide that will help inform and guide future design decisions as you are working.

RESETTING STYLES

Although we see the final results as fully styled text and design, Web pages are really just text files with HTML and CSS code applied to provide style and structure. Each browser interprets that code, and **renders** the page by applying **default** styles to your designs before your styles are applied using CSS code. However, different browser brands and even different versions do not agree precisely on exactly what those defaults should be, leading to slight inconsistencies.

The most popular method of dealing with this is to add a **CSS reset** to your code. The exact CSS reset you choose will depend on the needs of your design. We like to keep our reset simple, relying on adding styles to specific tags as needed. However, there are several styles that are inconsistent or (in our opinion) poorly set in most browsers.

Far too many Web sites are designed by default. The designers and developers allow the browser manufacturer to have the final word on how the content is displayed. By forcing you to set your styles, a good CSS reset can keep you from dull vanilla designs.

The argument for redefining important CSS properties (generally to none or zero) are straightforward:

- **Reduces bad styles**: Undoes some of the questionable and downright annoying styles added by browser manufacturers as well as the styles that simply do not work. One that springs to mind is using an outline to highlight items that are in focus such as form fields. While highlighting is useful for keyboard navigation, you should design this yourself.

- **Eliminates design by default**: Sets a level playing field from which to begin a design. Rather than allowing the browser manufacturers dictate how your pages look, you are now in control.

- **Browser style consistency**: Ensures values across all browser types and versions are the same. Since browsers vary their default style values slightly, a good reset will allow your designs to appear with greater consistency, regardless of how your visitor is viewing your site.

There are also several counter arguments to be made against a global reset, although we find their logic to be flawed.

- **Download time**: Adds more code and thus more load time. This is a stretch though, since the amount of added code will be small and by resetting the styles in a single place, you are likely eliminating repetition of the same definition in multiple selectors and thus reducing the amount of code.

- **Redundancy**: Many of the styles will simply be overwritten by styles later in the cascade. While possibly true, many styles will not be changed, so the global reset, while redundant in some cases, fills the gaps for the majority.

- **Rendering time**: Applying styles globally to every tag puts a burden on the browser's rendering engine. This is mostly an argument against using the universal selector (*), which would apply the styles to every single tag. However, I have not seen any data showing exactly what this lag would be, and haven't found any noticeable degradation in our tests, even on complex pages.

WHAT TO RESET

We recommend resetting many of the typographic and box styles and then setting selected defaults. Beyond not allowing the browser to set the direction, another good argument for resetting styles is that different browsers will have slightly different values

- **Padding, borders, and margins**: These are the main styles that designers like to reset, most because these vary so much from browser to browser.

- **Text underlining**: There is no good reason to ever use the text-decoration property to underline text. I have never seen a design where this property didn't do anything more than simply add visual noise, even for links. That is not to say that there is never a case where text should be underlined. Underlining text, though, is much better handled using the border-bottom property. Border-bottom gives more precise control, allowing you to specify the thickness, color and line style of the underline.

- **Line height:** The default for line height on text is 1 em, which means the text has little or no breathing room. All text can benefit from bumping this up a bit to at least 1.2 em and body copy can go higher to 1.5 em or higher.

- **Outlines**: Outlines are applied by some browsers such as Safari to highlight elements like form fields when they come into focus. While this is a good idea, this highlight should be up to you, not the browser.

- **Vertical alignment**: Vertical alignment is tricky and rarely works the way you expect it to. The best thing to do is set the vertical alignment to the baseline and then use relative positioning to move elements up or down from there manually.

- **Other**: These are the basics, but most CSS resets will go beyond them, cleaning up other perceived problems, generally with specific tag implementation. We'll look at them a little later in this chapter.

Text decoration only allows the line to be solid and the same color as the text with which it is used. CSS3 has added the ability to change the color and line type for text decoration, but this is still not fully supported in most browsers.

HOW TO RESET

Which of the many different CSS global resets you choose will depend on the needs of your particular project; however, we recommend keeping them as simple as you can: just reset what you need.

Resetting values is really a misnomer; All you are actually doing is setting styles for the HTML on your page, overriding the browser's default styles.

- **Keep it simple**: Don't reset styles unless you need them reset. If the browser defaults are not causing a problem, then it's okay to leave them.

- **Keep it compressed**: You are adding extra code that you are unlikely to want to change. You will need to take out all spaces, tabs, and line breaks.

- **Keep it at the top**: Since a reset is meant to override the browser default styles and not interfere with your other styles, always make sure that the override comes first in the cascade order.

There are two basic ways of resetting all of the styles, either by using the universal CSS selector, which is simpler, or by listing each tag individually, which is more backward compatible.

A SIMPLE CSS RESET

The easiest way to reset styles is with the universal selector and setting the default styles you want applied to all tags. The advantage of using the universal selector, other than compactness, is that it will always apply itself to new HTML tags as they become available;

```
* {  margin: 0;
     padding: 0;
     border: 0;
     outline: 0;
     font-size: 100%;
     font: inherit;
     line-height: 1.2em;
     vertical-align: baseline;
     text-decoration: none; }
```

ERIC MEYER'S CSS RESET

Beyond the simple custom CSS reset, the most commonly deployed CSS reset in general usage is the one devised by Eric Meyer. Created in response to a CSS reset code created by Yahoo!, Eric's reset attempted to not only clear the decks, but ensure that older browsers agreed on the newer HTML5 elements. Consult the page http://meyerweb.com/eric/tools/css/reset/ for more details, and to download the most recent version of Eric Meyer's CSS reset.

STYLE GUIDES

A style guide is simply a record of the styles used in a particular site or product, that can be easily shared with your client, team, or future designers and developers. A style guide can take many forms, including paper or electronic document, but the most effective style guides for the web are those that actually make use of the medium, and are built using CSS and HTML. This ensures that the styles will work the way you expect them to. Additionally, having an HTML/CSS style guide allows you to test the basic styles in various browsers and devices, is more easily updatable than paper, and more easily shared, since it is just another Web page.

WHAT TO INCLUDE IN A STYLE GUIDE

Every shop has its own specifics for what goes in the style guide, but here are the most commonly included elements:

- **Branding**: This can include the appropriate logo usage, with links to download the image for different uses. It should also include the brand's color palette, which may or may not be the same as the product color palette.

- **Product color palette**: Colors that can be used in this product in addition to the colors used for the brand include a color chip showing the color plus the Hex, RGB, and HSL values in a format that can be easily copied.

- **Product typeface**: Again, this may be in addition to or in place of any typefaces defined for the brand, but should reflect any and all typefaces and styles that are acceptable, along with a description of their general use in the design. See chapter 4 for a list of the type of types you will want to specify in this list.

- **Image recommendations**: Although you cannot include all of the images for the site, you want to include examples and guidelines for the kinds of images you need such as figures, diagrams, graphs, and any other visual information content. You should consider acceptable image dimensions, file sizes, styles, and general placement.

- **Iconography and labels**: Icons may or may not be used for all designs, but if used, should be included with instructions on how to use, and specific how icons are to be used for specific purposes. Additionally, labels used with or in place of icons in the design should be specified.

- **Refer to Chapter 8 for more details on iconography**

- **All HTML elements**: These are the essentials of a Web-based style guide, where you should include an example of every HTML5 tag available. Although it may seem like overkill since this will likely include tags that you rarely or never use, it prevents the designer from overlooking any elements. For example, designers often forget to design elements like the block quote or table footer. Including these in the style guide ensures a satisfied developer, product manager, and/or client who will not have to guess what these should look like if they do need to use them. Also, when changes are made to the CSS, they will be instantly reflected and can be checked in this part of the style guide.

- **UI patterns**: In addition to the HTML elements, any standard UI elements that you will be using in the product should be detailed. You might include things like progress bars and loader images, and even show common interface elements such as pagination, navigation menus, image sliders, and other controls. If you use the UI pattern more than once in the product, it probably belongs on this list.

- **Dos and don'ts**: Finally, a collection of what is permitted and not permitted in the design should be included. Don't be afraid to iterate this list, , throughout the design process and beyond, adding, subtracting, and editing it as needed.

CREATING A LIVING STYLE GUIDE

I highly recommend creating the style guide using HTML, CSS, and JavaScript. These are the technologies that will be used to actually deliver the design, and by using the core Web technologies you make it easier to share and maintain a living style guide. Once committed to paper, the style guide becomes static and will quickly go out of date as the design moves on and is changed.

- **Code snippets**: Provide a quick, clickable control that allows the user to view and copy code snippets for the HTML used for particular HTML and UI elements, and to download logos, images, and copy color values. This can make the style guide indispensable while protoyping new ideas.

- **Notes**: The ability for any viewer to add notes to the style guide turns the style guide into a forum where questions can be asked and suggestions for improvement made.

- **Downloadable and printable**: Although the living style guide is better, many users will want to be able to print the style guide for quick and constant reference without having to be online. Make sure to accommodate their needs.

- **Poster format for important elements**: We like to boil the style guide down to a few of the most important elements—color palette, iconography, typefaces—and turn that into an 11 × 17 poster to keep handy for reference.

STYLING WEIGHT

If you are only familiar with typography through a word processor, the concept of making text bold will seem straightforward—text is either darker (bold) or it is not (regular). However, typefaces will often include a wide variety of weights ranging from thin to heavy.

There is more than just one version of bold, but not all of them are always available. For the most part, font weights are specified as either bold (darker) or normal (regular). However, OpenType fonts can specify numeric weights ranging from 100 to 900 at increments of 100 (i.e., there is a font weight of 300, but not a font weight of 367). Each of these weights will correspond to a specific weight name or names used by the font. For example, if the font's name is Myriad Pro Light, then it will corresponds to a weight value of 300 or less. Additionally, fonts can be weighted relative to their parent element's font weight, either lighter or heavier.

Unfortunately, there are some browser inconsistencies with using numeric and relative values. The CSS standard states that if a numeric value is applied for which there is no font (i.e., the weight is not available for the typeface or its corresponding named weight), the browser should use the closest available weight. This is what the browsers do, although they can sometimes disagree on exactly which value is the "closest." There is also some discrepancy

Weight

Weight

Weight

Weight

Weight

S

When you apply an italic style to text, while lacking the italic or oblique version of the typeface, the browser automatically synthesizes the italic version for you. This synthesized text is pixelated, and rather difficult to read.

between how lighter and bolder selections act on a font weight, especially between Internet Explorer and other primary browsers.

Other than the browser inconsistencies, another obvious problem with using more than just the basic bold weight is that, if the font does not have the specified weight, the browser is likely to use the standard bold version, synthesize the weight, or use no weight change at all. Coupled with the fact that none of the core Webfonts and cross-OS Web-safe fonts don't have anything other than the basic bold, multiple weights are rarely used. However, now that downloadable fonts are more common, designers will be able to make use of a wider variety of font weights.

STYLING ITALIC AND OBLIQUE FONTS

In CSS, font style refers to whether a typeface uses an italic or oblique version. This style is often used to indicate that the text is a citation to another work or simply to add emphasis to a piece of text. In typography, normal text is referred to as the Roman face (also called regular) in contrast to the italic face. Oblique type is referred to as sloped Roman.

OBLIQUE IS NOT ITALIC, BUT THE TERMS ARE OFTEN USED INTERCHANGEABLY

Italic fonts were originally developed as more script or cursive looking alternatives within a typeface family, created as unique glyphs, stylistically similar, but distinct from the roman version. Italic fonts have the added benefit of being slanted, usually taking up less vertical space, and therefore allowing tighter printing.

Oblique type is often confused with italic, because they are both set at an angle and are used interchangeably in typography. However, unlike italics, an oblique font is not a unique glyph, but simply the Roman face slanted at an angle of anywhere from 2 degrees up to 20 degrees, but generally slanted around 10 degrees.

While not an absolute rule, seriffed typefaces will often include an italic version while sansserif fonts will use oblique. This is true of some sansserif typefaces even if the font is called italic and is actually a slanted Roman version with no unique glyphs.

In theory, when you refer to an oblique font in your CSS, you should get slanted Roman type, regardless of what fonts are available in the typeface. In practice however, browsers will always use the italic version of a font if it is available, regardless of whether you specify italic or oblique for the font style. If neither an oblique or italic version of the typeface is available, the browser will synthesize one, which is generally undesirable for quality typography.

STYLING COLOR

The most primal response we have to visual stimuli is in response to color. We associate colors with an ever-shifting series of concepts including religious, cultural, political, social, emotional and scientific. Yet, despite this instinctual understanding of the meaning of colors—or possibly because of it—color proves elusively difficult for many to use effectively in design.

The challenge that designers at all levels face is not just knowing which colors work best together, but also knowing how to restrain their use. The first lesson learned in color theory class is that "No color is better than bad color."

COLOR VALUES

A pixel's color value is defined as a combination of the primary colors—red, green, or blue—at different brightnesses and intensities. Most modern screens can display millions of different colors, defined by combinations of those primary colors.

Table 5.X shows the different ways to specify a color for use in Web design, mostly by combining RGB values from darkest to lightest. A new color value type available in Safari and Firefox is the RGB alpha value which allows you to set the transparency of the color from zero (clear) to 1 (opaque). However, RGBA does not work with hex color values. In Web typography, colors are set in four main place described on the next pages:

TEXT COLOR

Affects only the text color.

BACKGROUND

This sets the color of the background of the body or an element in the design. Backgrounds can also include images, where the colors can be solid or stochastic.

BORDER AND OUTLINE

Includes both a color value and style. Borders occupy space in the design, while the outline does not and cannot be rounded using the border radius property.

TEXT SHADOW AND BOX SHADOW

The shadow properties can have their colors set, allowing for a variety of effects. The box can have a shadow set both around it and inside it.

CHOOSING YOUR COLOR PALETTE

When considering color in typography, we have to stretch our consideration of the design from the individual glyphs that make up blocks of text to consider how that text interacts with the elements around that text—images and backgrounds.

When considering what colors to use, there are several tried-and-true combinations that work consistently, based on their placement within a color wheel. Five characteristics as listed below can be combined.

ANALOGOUS

Matching colors with adjacent hues.

MONOCHROMATIC

A single color with varied intensity and brightnesses. This is the simplest to use well, and is recommended if you are unsure how to work with color.

TRIAD

Three colors and their tones, separated in a triangular shape in the color wheel.

COMPLEMENTARY

Two colors from opposite sides of the color wheel, providing the highest contrast of any of the combinations.

SHADES

A single color with varied brightness.

TYPE EFFECTS

Unlike other typographic styles, text decoration styles do not change the individual characters, but are applied equally across a block of text. While there are currently only a few limited text decorations, and I recommend avoiding most of them, new decorations are on the way in CSS.

DO NOT USE UNDERLINE TO UNDERLINE LINKS

While underlining is the default style given to links and it is certainly true that users have been proven to respond to text that is underlined as hypertext links, the underline style is a crude and unattractive way to emphasize text. Underline places a rule (line) 1 px below the baseline of the text in the same color as the link, adding visual noise to the design, and obscuring any character descenders.

Additionally, not all links are created equal, and simply underlining a large list of links does little more than simply add clutter, interfering with scanability. Although adding white space can improve this, there is a better way to underline links, that I'll explain later in this chapter. Turn underlining off for all links and then add the underlining selectively, depending on context.

One other place that underline is used is with book titles, but that's a holdover from typewriters, and book titles should now be italicized, leaving underline without a use.

USING BORDERS OR BACKGROUNDS INSTEAD OF TEXT DECORATION

Instead of using the default link style, try using borders to style a customized underline with control over stroke weight and color. You can also apply a dash or dot to the stroke.

```
border-bottom: 1px solid red;
```

TEXT CASE

Text should already be set in the correct case by the system, but there will be times when you are not sure what case the text will be—for example, if it is dynamically provided by a database—or where you might want to change the case for emphasis, such as in header text.

Some fonts include a title case version for all capitals.

STYLING TEXT WITH BORDERS AND BACKGROUNDS

CREATING SPECIAL TEXT EFFECTS

TEXT SHADOW

The drop shadow treatment allows for some customization, including x and y coordinates. These values set the beginning of the shadow effect. The radius of the blur specifies how far the shadow extends from the letter form. Finally, the color value obviously determines the color of the shadow.

LETTER PRESS AND EMBOSS

This style gives your type an old-fashioned look; letter forms are shadowed to give the illusion of being bumped off the page or embossed into it. As with text shadowing, you can set the x and y coordinates, and blur distance and colors for the shadow.

3D TEXT

The 3D effect makes your text pop off the page by rendering each character with shadows, midtones, and highlights. This too requires a level of customization and you'll have to enter values for a wider range of shading.

BLURRED TEXT

This is a treatment that was once reserved for Photoshop, but now it can be achieved with CSS. The blur effect speaks for itself. You can customize the colors and blur radius for your needs. Blurring can be applied over a solid color or graduate to transparency over a photographic background.

GLOWING TEXT

Similar to blur, this effect creates a glow around selected letter forms. It can also add some interactivity to hover events. You just set your offsets, color and shadow distance and achieve a neon style without generating an image.

TRANSPARENT OVERLAP

This is a semiopaque box that helps text visually pop off the background. It is ideal for image captions, statements, and sidebars.

GRADIENT TEXT

This gives your headlines a glossy or metallic feel, depending on what colors you specify in your code.

TEXT TRANSFORMATIONS

This sets the case for your page's copy. The code can set your copy to all upper case or all lower case. It can also capitalize the first letter of each word.

ACCESSIBILITY

WEB CONTENT ACCESSIBILITY GUIDELINES (WCAG)

Font Selections
Wider character strokes can aid readability, and an overall bolder typeface can too.

Color Considerations
Color can affect readability for the vision impaired, making it difficult to separate text from the background. Therefore, high contrast color palettes can assist with this issue.

Resolution Considerations
Using text within an image should be avoided because pixelation can cause illegibility for the vision impaired. For font sizing, an 18 point body weight or 14 point bold face is deemed adequate.

Dyslexia and Dysgraphia
Because reading strains the eyes, you should make your site as easy to navigate as possible, and such considerations as links in copy will be greatly appreciated. Tables and lists can also help the users find the information they desire.

source http://www.w3.org/TR/UN-DERSTANDING-WCAG20/visual-audio-contrast-contrast.html

STYLE CHECKLIST

- Does your font have an italic or oblique version of all weights, widths, and styles?

- Does the font's voice match the project and/or the tone of your client?

- Does your typeface have the needed glyphs for your project?

- Many Webfont services allow you to test run sample text for auditioning your font.

- Can the font grow with your project? Some typefaces become overused and this is a consideration.

SCALE

6

There is no such thing as an
empty space or an empty time.
There is always something to
see, something to hear. In fact,
try as we may to make a silence,
we cannot.

John Cage

The carpenter's adage is "Measure twice, cut once." Giving careful consideration to the measurements and scale you are designing for is what separates good Web typography from great typography. Size and space add texture and flow to your text, improving the readability and clarity of what you are trying to say.

When typographers talk about "motion" in type, they are describing the way that a well composed text will compel the reader's eye, moving it along from the beginning to the end with as little disruption as possible.

Many designers want to define with exact precision the placement and size of elements, similar to the way they might design for print or video. Those media are static, while video might move and be projected on to larger screens, the aspect ratio does not change so all elements scaled relatively. However, on the Web, you are dealing with a variable canvas, with its final size dependent on the whims of the reader.

abcdefghijklmnopqrstuvwxyz
CHUBBET DISTENDED

UNDERSTANDING RELATIVE AND ABSOLUTE TYPE UNITS

Keep in mind that although some units are traditionally associated with typography (like points and picas) and others with measurements of distance (like inches or centimeters), all units are available to set any size or dimension. For example, you can set your font size in millimeters or the padding on a column in picas.

In Web design, sizes can either be expressed in absolute or relative terms. We explain later in this section which to use for a particular situation, but will first review the different measurement types and the units at your disposal.

Absolute value units (*Table 6.1*) are used to precisely control sizes, so that they do not vary regardless of the particular screen size, browser, or operating system used. Even absolute units can vary between computers, generally because of the operating system. This was the case with point sizes between Mac and Windows.

Relative value units (*Table 6.2*) have no fixed size, but instead are calculated relative to another value, such as the parent element's size or to the screen dimensions. Although less precise, relative values have the advantage that they can be quickly scaled for the screen and changed without having to recalculate all of their dependent values. For example, if you are using relative values to set the font size and line height, simply changing the font size will also change the line height proportionally.

unit	name	description	example
pt	point	72 pt = 1 inch	12 pt
pc	pica	1 pc = 12 pt	1 pc
mm	millimeter	1 mm = .24 pc	4.17 mm
cm	centimeter	1 cm = 10 mm	.42 cm
in	inch	1 in = 2.54 cm	.17 in

Table 6.1

Absolute Value Units

unit	name	description	example
%	percent	relative to size of parent element	150%
em	em	relative to parent element 1 em = 100%	1.5 em
rem	rem	relative to body element	
ex	x-height	from baseline to top of lowercase x in font	4.17 mm
px	pixel	relative to monitor resolution	12 px

Table 6.2

Relative Value Units

USE POINTS FOR PRINT BUT NEVER FOR SCREEN

Although standard for print design, point sizes are discouraged for use when defining font sizes for use on screens. The problem comes down to an inconsistency between Mac and Windows monitor resolution settings.

By definition, a point is 1/72 of an inch, or 72 points per inch (ppi). A Mac computer assumes a monitor resolution of 72 dots per inch (dpi), which also coincides with the number of points per inch. On the other hand, Windows computers assume your monitor displays 96 dpi. If the system is set for large fonts, Windows compounds the problem and assumes 120 dpi. Unix systems can vary between 75 and 100 dpi. These assumptions by the operating systems result in a Macintosh using 18 pixels to render 18 point text, a Windows system typically uses 24 pixels, a Unix system typically uses between 19 and 25 pixels, and a Windows system using a large font setting uses 30 pixels.

The upshot is that most Windows users see text that is 33% larger than text on a Macintosh if set using point sizes, rendering points all but useless for Web design on screen. While most Mac browsers will try to adjust for this problem by increasing the base Mac font size to 16, some variance will persist.

However, if you are designing a Web page for print (i.e., media="print"), using point sizes is not only perfectly acceptable, it is the preferred method for defining precise font sizes.

USE PIXELS FOR PRECISION CONTROL, BUT KNOW THAT YOU ARE TAKING CONTROL FROM THE USER

Although it is possible to precisely control the position of elements with any of the absolute units, pixels are the most natural way to define measurements for screen-based media. Despite being a "relative" size, pixels behave absolutely in context to the screen resolution, and many modern Web design today will be specified in pixels because they are the most universal measurements regard-

Pixel Mosaic

All images on the screen (fonts included) are composed of a mosaic of tiny dots called pixels.

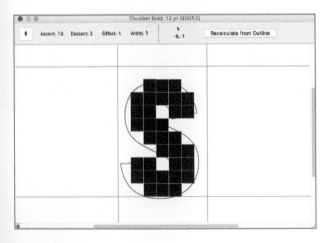

less of screen size, OS, or browser. Like atoms in molecules, pixels are irreducible as the smallest units of meaningful distance on the screen—you can't move something half a pixel.

While pixels give the designer precise control over where elements appear, they are not without their issues and inconsistencies. Most Web browsers allow users to enlarge text and zoom the page size, which is imperative for anyone with poor vision. Locking the font size with pixels or absolute values prevents Internet Explorer from changing their size. Internet Explorer 7 rectifies this limitation somewhat by allowing the entire page to be zoomed, but there is still some debate over pixel use when accessibility is an issue.

USE EMS AND PERCENTAGES FOR FLUID DESIGN

In order to provide the reader with highest level of control over the content to be viewed, it is increasingly considered a best practice to define sizes (both font sizes and other length measurements) using relative units, especially ems.

The em (pronounced "m") is the fundamental unit of measurement in typography which is defined as the size of the type as computed relative to the current size of the type of the parent element. For example, if you set the font size of your Web page to 12 px, then .5 em = 6 PX; 1em = 12 px; 1.5 em = 18 px; 2em = 24 px. If you change the font size to 14 px, then .5 em = 7 px; 1 em = 14 px; 1.5 em = 21 px; 2 em = 28 px. Ems work like percentage values for the purpose of font sizing. However, percentages and ems work differently for margins and padding, with percentages based on the parent width or height and ems based on the parent em size.

One reason that ems are not popular for general use becomes obvious: since their computed size is relative to their parent's size, you have to keep track of the current parent size to know how large or small the font will appear.

Despite their complexity, the advantage of using ems is that you can quickly change the scale of your design by simply changing a single font-size value. Since ems are relative to the parent's font size, changing the parent's value changes the values for all of its children. Additionally, since some older browsers, most notably IE 6, will not resize text set in points, using ems guarantees that all of your readers get the same experience.

The bottom line is that whether you use pixels or ems is up to you. I recommend keeping them consistent within a document to avoid confusion.

TYPE SIZE AND LINE HEIGHT

In Web design, type size is set using one of two CSS properties, either font which is a shortcut to set several different font values or font-size which is only used to set the size. The space between lines of text in a block can also be set in the font property or by using the line-height property.

Any of the relative or absolute size value units listed earlier in this chapter can be applied to set the font size or line height as well as specific keywords that are used to set absolute sizes and can be adjusted with relative size keywords. Line height can also be set as a numeric value, without any units, setting the spacing between lines as a multiple of the font size.

UNDERSTAND HOW TYPE IS MEASURED

A typeface height is measured from the cap height (the height of the tallest capital letter) to the descender with some breathing room added at the bottom to prevent characters on different lines from overrunning each other. The exact bottom buffer is set by the type designer. Taller uppercase letters—b, d, f, h, i, k, l, and t— will often rise slightly above the cap height, but are not included in the measurement. Although each character in the font might have a different visual height, they occupy the same amount of space vertically, even if they do not fill it.

Even if set to the same size, a font's x-height will likely vary, leading to some fonts that look taller than others and often making them more readable, as is the case between Times and Georgia.

The width of a character is simply its visual width plus any space beside it. This space may vary from letter to letter and can be kerned—the process of adjusting letter spacing to optimize the legibility of that particular font. The exceptions to this are the monospace fonts, which will always occupy the same width regardless of the character.

SIZE FONTS WITH ABSOLUTE KEYWORDS FOR CONSISTENCY, BUT AVOID RELATIVE KEYWORDS

In addition to specific units of measurement, you can set font sizes using relative and absolute key words. The keywords are self-explanatory, as good keywords should be.

- **Absolute size keywords**—xx-small, x-small, small, medium, large, x-large, and xx-large—will set the type to a specific size as defined by the browser. Medium, is the default browser font size.

- **Relative size keywords**—smaller and larger— make text smaller or larger relative to its parent element's font size. Unfortunately, different browsers use different algorithms to determine the relative font size change, making them unreliable for browser interoperability.

As previously mentioned, each browser has a slightly different algorithm for computing relative sizes, so there is some browser variance, which is compounded when relative sizes are nested. Internet

Explorer and Firefox are the most consistent, but even they vary when using smaller font sizes.

Although the range for absolute keywords is limited, they allow you to quickly apply a set scale to your type. However, since relative font sizes are so inconsistently calculated between browsers, they are not recommended.

HORIZONTAL TYPE SPACE

One way to add variety to your text is through the use of spacing between characters and words. Although not for "everyday" use, adding or subtracting space in your type is an important tool for creating fluid typography.

LETTER SPACING IS NOT KERNING, BUT IT'S ALL WE'VE GOT

It's easy to confuse kerning with the practice of simply spacing characters farther apart or closer together. Kerning adjusts the spacing between characters in a proportional font; however, it will do this differently for different combinations of character pairs, allowing them to fit together optimally based on the font's own coordinate system. For example, the kerning applied to the letter pair WA is negative so that the A slides underneath the W, increasing their readability by reducing the optical space between them. The kerning for UA, on the other hand, is zero, since there is no room to comfortably adjust the optical space.

In digital typesetting, kerning is automatically set by the font, but can be adjusted. The base kerning between two characters is zeroand can be adjusted with values between −100 and 200 (there are no units associated) and applied to loosen or tighten the space between two or more letters in a block of text. Each letter will be affected differently by the values relative to the letters next to them.

In Web design, true kerning is not available. Instead, CSS offers the letter-spacing property to add tracking to text. Tracking is the ability to add a specific amount of space between each character. In theory, you could use this to adjust individual letters by placing span tags around one or more letters and then applying letter spacing.

In practice, though, this technique is all but unworkable since tags would have to be placed for every instance where kerning adjustment is needed.

Since different letters require different amounts of space added or removed to improve readability, and so much content on the Web is dynamically created or contributed by writers who may not be able to control the code, this technique is only applied in extreme circumstances.

USE LETTER SPACING AND WORD SPACING FOR EFFECT, BUT USE THEM SPARINGLY

Both letter spacing and word spacing are blunt typographic instruments, coarsely adding space, regardless of the specific text. In general, the fonts you use in your design will already be carefully kerned by the type designer to maximize readability. If not, you probably need to pick a different font, so letter spacing and word spacing should not be necessary to improve readability.

There are times when you may want to add space to draw attention to text or to differentiate it from surrounding text, especially in titles and headers. Since this is done as a stylistic flourish rather than to improve readability, there are no hard-and-fast rules for how much space to add based on your design needs. In order to ensure that the text is easily scalable without having to adjust the spacing if the font size is increased, use ems, which will always keep the same proportion at any font size.

SET LETTER SPACING FOR CAPITALIZED ABBREVIATIONS AND ACRONYMS

Letter spacing is often needed in abbreviations and acronyms, where the string of capital letters will be spaced out as if they were solitary letters, rather than as part of a group. If your HTML code is properly constructed, this should not be problem, as long as acronyms and abbreviations use the abbreviation tag.

CSS can then be used to style the abbreviation tag to tighten the spacing by 5% or five tenths of an em.

One potential issue is that not all abbreviations will need letter spacing. For example the abbreviation for et cetera (etc.) is lower case, and lower case letters do not require tightening. This may mean that you only apply the abbreviation to upper case abbreviations.

Additionally, you might choose to set a negative letter spacing for long strings of numbers, but this might be a challenge since there is no direct way to tag numbers in HTML without adding span tags around the numerals.

USE INDENTS OR SPACES BETWEEN PARAGRAPHS, BUT NOT BOTH

Traditionally, typographers separated paragraphs of text by indenting the first line of text by at least 1 em with the space between paragraphs equal to the line height. Additionally, the first lines of opening paragraphs in a section would not be indented.

When the Web was first developed, there was no way to set a paragraph indent, and multiple spaces were always collapsed into a single space. To differentiate paragraphs, Web content producers began to simply add extra margin space between paragraphs, visually separating them.

Despite the fact that CSS long ago introduced the ability to add paragraph indents, separating paragraphs with additional white space has become the default standard style on the Web.

All paragraphs of text will already be separated by the space of the line height. To calculate the optimal extra margin to be added, multiply your line height by .75:

```
line height x 0.75 = paragraph spacing.
```

If your line height is 24 px, the optimal margin would be 18 px. In theory, you should either add this to the top or bottom margin of the paragraph. However, one feature of modern Web browsers is that they will *collapse* top and bottom margins between elements, using the larger value as the only margin between the elements, ignoring the smaller value. Known as margin collapsing, this means that you not only can, but should set the margin for the tops and bottoms of paragraphs, generally to the same value.

This also ensures that the first and last paragraph in your body copy can have top and bottom margins. The above code renders a total space between paragraphs of 42 px as measured form baseline to baseline.

If you want to use indents, you will need to remove the margins between paragraphs and add the desired indent, generally equal to twice the current font size or larger. If this is the first paragraph in a section, you will not want an indent.

This will help with the scanability of the text, especially if you use a separate style for the first character and/or first line of text at the start of a section.

TEXT ALIGNMENT

Text alignment is generally taken for granted on the Web—left alignment suits most purposes most of the time. In order to create a sense of rhythm and movement on your page, helping move the reader's eye around and adding visual interest to the page, a little alignment variation can go a long way.

SET BODY TEXT ALIGNMENT TO MINIMIZE GAPS AND MAXIMIZE SCANNING

Text alignment in Web pages is, by default, to the left, with ragged edges on the right. Although justified text—sometimes called "newspaper columns" because both edges of the text are aligned—can be deployed, this is rare on the Web.

In print, justified text is created using a variety of techniques including word spacing, letter spacing, hyphenation, and glyph reshaping. In addition, well formed justification is calculated on a paragraph level to prevent "rivers" of white space flowing down the middle. On the Web, unfortunately, justification is simply created by adding small amounts of space between words. On the screen, which can only add whole pixels, this tends to lead to uncomfortably large amounts of space between some words, especially in narrower columns.

When choosing to use left or justified alignment, keep in mind these factors:

- Justified text is often seen as more formal and structured looking while left alignment is more informal and approachable.

- Justified text will reinforce the grid structure of a page, but can be harder to scan since it often creates rivers of white space throughout the text, interrupting the eye path.

- Left aligned text adds an element of white space to the right edge softening the overall appearance of the page.

CENTER OR RIGHT JUSTIFY TEXT FOR EFFECT AND VARIETY

More rarely used, centering or right justifying text is primarily used to create a specific feeling on the page.

Centering and right aligning text will be integrally dependent on the design you are creating and how you want your readers to scan the page. While using a variety of justifications helps create a rhythm and motion on your page, the material can quickly become cluttered or obnoxious. Always have a specific purpose for the variance of alignment, and use it sparingly. Here are a few ideas:

- Bulleted or numbered lists should not be centered or right aligned as this makes them harder to scan by moving the beginning of each line around.

- Center section or module titles and headers if you want to make your site look a little different. Generally, section titles are best left aligned, but can be centered to give your designs a unique feel and possibly improve scanability.

- Right align text in the left column of a page or table if it helps show a closer relationship between the elements in adjacent columns.

INCREASE MARGINS FOR LONGER QUOTATIONS AND STYLE CITATIONS

Shorter quotes of less than three lines are included in a paragraph and surrounded by quotation marks, requiring no other special formatting. In HTML, the blockquote tag is used to separate a block of text as a quotation, generally two lines of text or more. The quotation should be styled to distinguish it from other text by indenting its left and right margins and increasing the top and bottom margins. The amount of left and right indentation will be based on the width of the column and then adjusted so as not to conflict with any other indents. A good measure to offset blockquotes is double the fonts size (2 em), although more or less space may be required for wider or narrower columns.

This will clearly space the blockquote away from the rest of the text, but it's also up to the copy writer to make it clear that the text is a quote and to supply its source, possibly using a cite tag, which is used to indicate a quote. We recommend turning the cite tag into a block level element and right aligning it when it is included in a blockquote.

The above code will force any text marked by a citation tag to a new line and right align it.

SET FOOTNOTES AND SCIENTIFIC OR MATHEMATICAL ANNOTATIONS USING POSITIONING RATHER THAN VERTICAL ALIGNMENT

Vertical text alignment allows you to adjust the position of inline text in relation to its natural baseline, shifting it up or down. For footnotes, mathematics and scientific notation, it will not be enough to simply raise or lower character; you will also need to reduce its size relative to the surrounding text. These styles can be applied to the superscript or subscript tags, setting the vertical position to the baseline, and then setting a position relative to that.

Although vertical align provides several values to set the vertical position of the text, these have proven to be unreliable in multi-column layouts. The exact values will vary depending on the font, and you may also need to add some left or right margins to add breathing room.

CRIPT

MONOSPACE

HUMANIST

ETRO

X

GEOME

FIXED W

SPACE

7

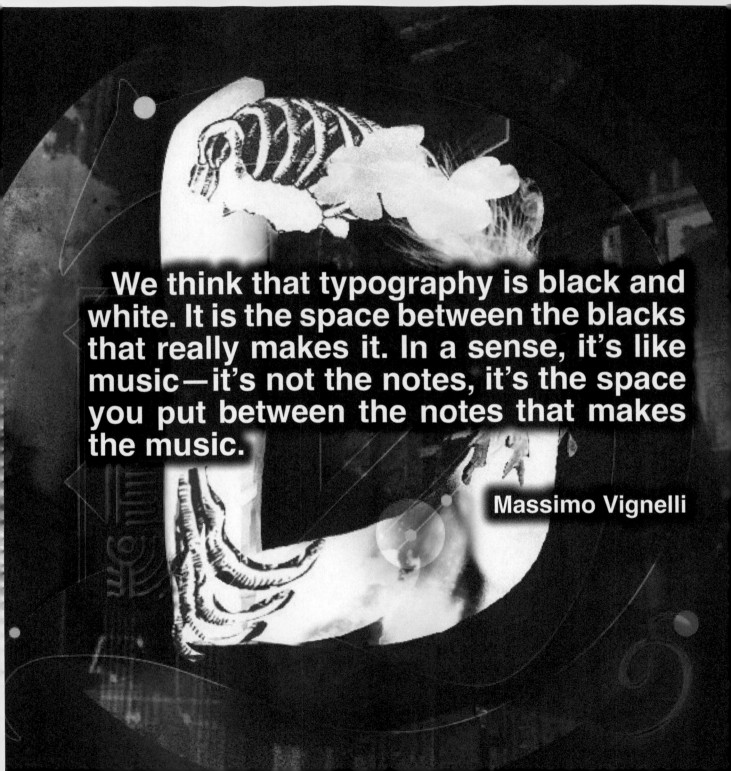

We think that typography is black and white. It is the space between the blacks that really makes it. In a sense, it's like music—it's not the notes, it's the space you put between the notes that makes the music.

Massimo Vignelli

Like the silences in music, it's the space between and around type that creates meaning. For the most part, we tend to leave the space defaults in place, and rarely adjust spaces between letters, between words, between lines of text, and between paragraphs. Unfortunately, design by default all too often controls the space (line lenths) that space occupies, leading to lines of text that stretch uncomfortably across wide screens or are crammed into narrow screens, rather than fitting attractively to the space available.

Like a conductor controlling the ebb and flow of music (both sounds and silences), the job of typographers is to not only control the appearance of letters, but also the spaces between them and their lengths. For the Web, this takes on a whole new meaning when you recognize that the spacing you are designing can vary greatly from reader to reader, and might even shift while being read.

abcdefghijklmnopqrstuvwxyz
HELVETICA BOLD

VERTICAL TYPE SPACE

Choose a line height that gives your body copy breathing room. Beyond the size of the text, one of the most frequently overlooked factors in creating readable text is the line height and the width of the column in proportion to the line height. It's important to stress that line height is not the space between lines of text—as it is often mistakenly thought of—but the space from the base line of one line of text to the baseline of the next line of text.

A minimum font size to line height ratio of 2 to 3 is recommended for any extensive body copy:

Body font size × 1.5 = line height

A font size of 16 px would require a line height of 24 px or higher. To simplify matters, you could simply apply a line height of 1.5 em, 150%, or simply set a numerical value of 1.5. All of these will add the correct line height, regardless of how the copy is re-sized.

In addition to font size, column width will also affect the optimal line height. Narrow columns and shallower blocks of text, like headers, require less line height to be quickly scannable, generally reducing the font size to line height ratio as low as 1:1.125. However, to preserve a more uniform page grid, designers will keep the line height consistent regardless of the column width and use font, style, and color changes to better differentiate columns. Use Indents or spaces between paragraphs, but not both

Traditionally, typographers separated paragraphs of text by indenting the first line of text by at least 1 em with the space between paragraphs equal to the line height. Additionally, the first line of opening paragraphs in a section would not be indented.

When the Web was first developed, there was no way to set a paragraph indent, and multiple spaces were always collapsed into a single space. To differentiate paragraphs, Web content producers began to simply add extra margin space between paragraphs, visually separating them.

Despite the fact that CSS long ago introduced the ability to add paragraph indents, separating paragraphs with additional white space has become the default standard style on the Web.

All paragraphs of text will already be separated by the space of the line height. To calculate the optimal extra margin to be added, multiply your line height by .75:

```
'line height x 0.75 = paragraph spacing'
```

If your line height is 24 px, the optimal margin would be 18 px. In theory, you should either add this to the top or bottom margin of the paragraph. However, one feature of modern Web browsers is that they will collapse top and bottom margins between elements, using the larger value as the only margin between the elements, ignoring the smaller value. Known as margin collapsing, this means that you can and should set the margin for the tops and bottoms of paragraphs, generally to the same value:

```
<p style="margin-top: 18px;">
```

This also ensures that the first and last paragraph in your body copy can have top and bottom margins. The above code renders a total space between paragraphs of 42 px as measured from base line to baseline.

If you want to use indents, you will need to remove the margins between paragraphs and add the desired indent, generally equal to twice the current font size or larger. If this is the first paragraph in a section, you will not want an indent:

```
p{

    text-indent: 50px;

}
```

This will help with the scanability of the text, especially if you use a separate style for the first character and/or first line of text at the start of a section.

TEXT ALIGNMENT

Text alignment is generally taken for granted on the Web—left alignment suits most purposes most of the time. In order to create a sense of rhythm and movement on your page, helping move the reader's eye around and adding visual interest to the page, a little alignment variation can go a long way.

Set body text alignment to minimize gaps and maximize scanning text alignment in Web pages is, by default, to the left, with ragged edges on the right. Although justified text—sometimes called "newspaper columns" where both edges of the text are aligned—can be deployed, but this is rare on the Web.

In print, justified text is created using a variety of techniques including word spacing, letter spacing, hyphenation, and glyph reshaping. In addition, well formed justification is calculated on a paragraph level to prevent "rivers" of white space flowing down the middle. On the Web, unfortunately, justification is simply created by adding small amounts of space between words. On the screen, which can only add whole pixels, this tends to lead to uncomfortably large amounts of space between some words, especially in narrower columns.

When choosing to use left or justified alignment, keep in mind these factors: Justified text is often seen as more formal and structured looking while left alignment is more informal and approachable. Justified text will reinforce the grid structure of a page, but can be harder to scan since it often creates rivers of white space throughout the text, interrupting the eye path. Left aligned text adds an element of white space to the right edge, softening the overall appearance of the page. Center or right justified text provides effect and variety.

Centering or right justifying text is occasionally used to create a specific feeling on the page. Centering and right aligning text will be integrally dependent on the design you are creating and how you want your readers to scan the page. While using a variety of justifications helps create a rhythm and motion on your page, the result can quickly become cluttered or obnoxious. Always have a specific purpose for the variance of alignment, and use it sparingly. Here are a few ideas:

Bulleted or numbered lists should not be centered or right aligned as this makes them harder to scan. Center section or module titles and headers if you want to make your site look a little different. Generally, section titles are best left aligned, but can be centered in designs to give a unique feel and possibly improve scanability. Right align text in the left column of a page or table if it helps show a closer relationship between the elements in adjacent columns.

Increase margins for longer quotations and style the citation so shorter quotes of less than three lines are included in a paragraph and surrounded by quotation marks, requiring no other special formatting. In HTML, the blockquote tag is used to separate a block of text as a quotation, generally of two lines of text or longer. The quotation should be styled to distinguish it from other text by indenting its left and right margins and increasing the top and bottom margins. The amount of left and right indentation will be based on the width of the column and then adjusted so as not to conflict with other indents. A good measure to offset blockquotes is double the fonts size (2 em), although more or less space may be required for wider or narrower columns.

This will clearly space the blockquote away from the rest of the text, but it's also up to the copy writer to make it clear that the text is a quote and to supply its source, possibly using the tag, which is used to indicate a citation. We recommend turning the cite tag into a block level element and right aligning it when it is included in a blockquote:

```
block quote cite { display: block; text-align: right; }
```

The above code will force any text marked by the citation tag to a new line and right align it.

Set footnotes and scientific or mathematical annotations using positioning rather than vertical alignment.

Vertical text alignment allows you to adjust the position of inline text in relation to its natural baseline, shifting it up or down. For footnotes, mathematics and scientific notation, it will not be enough to simply raise or lower the character; you will also need to reduce their sizes relative to the surrounding text. These styles can be applied to the superscript or subscript tags, setting the vertical position to the baseline, and then setting a position relative to that:

Although vertical align provides several values to set the vertical position of the text, these values have proven unreliable in multi-column layouts. The exact values will vary, depending on the font, and you may also need to add some left and right margins to add breathing room.

LINE LENGTHS

One of the most common problems with on screen text is lines of text that stretch from one side of the screen to the other. For smaller screens, this isn't an issue, but if left unchecked on larger screens , the line lengths become downright annoying. Choose a column width that will not tire your readers.

In addition to considering the font size, another important consideration for readability is the column width. Reading slows the longer a column grows beyond a certain length. A comfortable column width will be easily derived by considering the font size. Although not an absolute requirement, column width is also dependent on the typeface used. A good rule to determine a comfortable column width is to multiply the font size by 28:

```
body font size × 28 ≈ column width.
```

This is a rough value, and the multiple might range anywhere between 25 and 33, depending on your preference. If we assume a font size of 16 px for our body copy, a comfortable column width will be around 450 px.

Again, ems can come to our rescue by allowing us to set columns based on the font size:

For a fluid design that makes optimal use of the available screen real estate, set the maximum and minimum column widths within the comfort range.

The column width expands or contracts as space is available within the Web design, but never stretch too wide or too narrow to ensure comfortable reading.

SET LETTER SPACING FOR CAPITALIZED ABBREVIATIONS AND ACRONYMS

Letter spacing is often needed in abbreviations and acronyms, where the strings of capital letters will be spaced out as if they were solitary letters, rather than as parts of a group. If your HTML code is properly constructed, this should not be problem, as long as acronyms and abbreviations use the abbreviation tag.

CSS can then be used to style the abbreviation tag to tighten the spacing by 5% or 5 tenths of an em.

One potential issue is that not all abbreviations need letter spacing. For example the abbreviation for et cetera (etc.) is lowe case, and lower case letters do not require tightening. This may mean that you only apply the abbreviation to upper case abbreviations.

Additionally, you might choose to set a negative letter spacing for long strings of numbers, but this might be a challenge since there is no direct way to tag numbers in HTML without adding a span tag around the numerals.

true type flavor

OPEN
TYPE
.woff

fl

ition

LINE

ICONOGRAPHY

8

I say, follow your bliss and don't be afraid,
and doors will open where you didn't know
they were going to be.

Joseph Campbell

The Power of Myth

Although modern syllabic languages are far more complex than hiero-glyphic languages used by the ancients, a well-placed pictogram (or icon) can still come in handy when you need to communicate complex ideas in a small space. The problem is that finding good icons—images that don't look like cheap clip art—can be daunting.

An icon is a simplified picture used to represent a concept or object. Icons often appear in a single flat color, but can become increasingly complex, and include photos in some cases, but it's important to keep icons as simple as possible to meet your site's needs.

Indeed, although individual icons can have simple meanings, combining icons allows them to take on more complex meanings and even tell stories — a capability that designers are increasingly utilizing.

abcdefghijklmnopqrstuvwxyz
PERPETUA BOLD

WHEN TO USE ICONS

If used with consideration, icons can dramatically improve your audiences' ability to scan, understand and remember what they've read.

Icons should always do one or more of the following:

» **Quickly and compactly convey concepts**: Controls such as "print," "save," "copy," and "paste" are often represented as icons to save the space that lengthier words need. Additionally, each icon is the same relative size and each concept receives the same visual emphasis, while words can be different lengths.

» **Draw attention and emphasize important ideas**: On a page full of text, icons at the beginnings of sections serve as visual organizers. They can help your reader quickly scan for the information sought on the page, without taking the time to read each section individually.

» **Provide a visual memory trigger**: Icons can also help readers remember underlying concepts by associating them with a visual meme. This cannot replace the underlying text, but by visualizing the icon after reading, some readers—especially visual learners—may be more likely to recall the associated concepts.

One caution about icons is that they lose their impact if overused. Always have a specific and targeted use for the icons you include.

CHOOSING ICONS

There are some obvious problems with icons, which is why we don't just chuck the alphabet and use them instead. Chief among these is interpretation—an icon should be easily understood by the audience with as little variance as possible. If readers have to spend any amount of time deciphering an icon or if different viewers get different meanings, the icon is not doing its job.

When considering what icon to use, remember that an icon must fulfill one or more of the following criteria to be successful:

1 **Common**: The meaning of the icon is generally universally known and accepted, even if that meaning is not intrinsic in its shape. For example, the hexagon is almost universally known for meaning "stop." One caution, though, is making sure your audience knows what an icon means, since meaning is often based on experience and culture.

2 **Recognizable**: The meaning is obvious without the context of any related text, generally because the icon has an easily identifiable shape that represents a real world object. For example, the icon of an umbrella—while not particularly common—is easily recognizable as long as it not made too abstract.

3 **Illustrative**: The icon should reinforce the meaning of the text, but may not be immediately obvious without it. This is especially true with instructional text, where the icons might be combined to show a process.

Icons can offer the designer the ability to train users, for example, think of Apple's Share icon, the box with the up-pointing arrow. Icons can help a brand develop its own visual language. They can help users answers questions, communicate, get more information on a product, purchase the product and quickly navigate your site. Always remember, the attention span of the average person is ever decreasing and anything you can do to streamline your site's navigational system is to your advantage.

Icons, like typefaces, can also be in-your face, edgy or subtle and reserved. Line quality , type design plays an important role in the development of an icon, its visual look, and feel. You can even draw your own graphic, and auto trace it in Illustrator to get a custom, hand -designed effect or quality that is unique to your site.

RESPONSIVE ICONS

One of the major problems we face in responsive Web design is how to create icons that scale to the interface, not just for physical dimensions, but based on screen size and number of pixels per inch. Generally, images are used to add icons in line using the <img> tag. Another common technique relies on a grid of the different icons and states—a CSS sprite—saved in a bitmap format, typically GIF or PNG.

However, the more you scale these images up or down to respond to the context, the more the icon will appear distorted as the bitmap image's anti-aliasing becomes increasingly apparent. Even worse, sprite-based icons cannot be reliably or easily scaled.

At its intrinsic size, and icon looks fine, but enlarge it—even just a little—and the edges blur where they have been anti-aliased. This is why many designers and developers avoid icons in their design, despite the fact that icons can be amazingly effective at communicating complex ideas in a limited space.

To create responsive designs with scalable icons, we recommend replacing bitmap image icons with vector-based Webfonts. These are infinitely scalable with no loss of fidelity. In this section, we show you how to use Webfonts to replace image-based icons in your design to improve accessibility, scalability and "style-ability."

The advantages of using Webfont icons fall into three distinct categories:

1. Accessible: Webfont icons can be used in place of HTML text. The trick is to hide the HTML text from human users, replacing it with the icon using CSS, but allowing it to be displayed for screen readers and search engines.

2. Scalable: Because they are rendered using a vector instead of a bitmap image, icons can be made as small or as large as possible without any loss of fidelity. This allows you to create more responsive designs where the icon size matches the needs of the interface.

3. Stylable: Because CSS is used to style the icons, they can be re-styled wherever and however you want without having to re-create new images every time. This also means that you can choose from a wide variety of CSS text effects that look attractive and dynamic.

USING WEBFONT ICONS

Webfont icons work by using CSS to inject a specific glyph into the HTML using the content property. Webfonts then use @font-face to load a dingbat Webfont that styles the injected glyph and that injected glyph becomes the desired icon.

To begin, you'll need a Webfont file with the icons you need, either defined for particular ASCII characters (A, B, C, !, @, #, etc.) or in the Private Use Area of the Unicode font, that provides spaces in the font that will not be used by specific characters in a Unicode-encoded font. Entypo provides free dingbat Webfonts.

1 Load the font file. Begin by defining your icon font file's path using the standard CSS @font-face rule (be sure you have uploaded these files to your server):

' @font-face { font-family: "icons"; src: url("fonts/icons.eot");

src: url("fonts/icons.eot?#iefix") format("embedded-opentype"),
```
url("fonts/icons.woff") format("woff"),
url("fonts/icons.ttf") format("truetype"),
url("fonts/icons.svg#icons") format("svg");
```

font-weight: normal; font-style: normal; }'

Make sure to include sources for TrueType, EOT, and WOFF formats. Also include the SVG version of the font. Although it is being rapidly replaced by the WOFF format, SVG is still needed for older iOS devices.

1 Create a CSS rule that turns any tag which contains a class with "icon-" in it into a receptacle for the icon. This selector allows you to add an icon to any tag you want using a class that contains the string "icon-":

```
[class*="icon-"] { background-image: none; dis-
play: inline; font-size: 1em; font-style: normal !im-
portant; font-weight: normal !important; height: 1em;
overflow: visible; width: 1em; }
```

We also need to set the font size, width and height of our icon to 1 em so that we can easily scale it using relative sizes. Also remove any possible font weights and styles, which would distort the icon if applied.

3: Create a selector that adds the icon to the receiving tag. Now comes the trick. We use the CSS content property to add a glyph before the tag, and then style that glyph using the icon font we set up in step 1.

```
[class*="icon-"]::before { content: '+'; display:
inline-block; font-family: "icons", fantasy !impor-
tant; line-height: 1; position: relative; top: 2px;
-webkit-font-smoothing: antialiased; font-smoothing:
antialiased; }
```

This will use the content property to add a default character—a plus sign—as a placeholder before the actual tag using the ::before pseudo-element. Additionally, it's a good idea to add the WebKit font-smoothing property. We've also added a W3C version of that property to be safe, but that property isn't approved yet.

4: Create a selector that hides content in the icon tag Create a class called hide that will hide any text you want to include for SEO and backward compatibility. Apply this class to any child element within the tag you are using to create the actual icon.

```
.hide { clip: rect(1px, 1px, 1px, 1px); height: 0;
opacity: 0; position: absolute; visibility: hidden;
width: 0; }
```

5: Create a CSS rule to add the specific glyph for the desired icon The final CSS selector is the actual icon you want to use, according to the letter that corresponds to the icon in your default set. The letter in this example, "t", is used for the Twitter icon.

```
.icon-twitter::before { content: "t"; }
```

In theory, you could also use ::after instead of ::before but if the icon is associated with text, generally you will want the icon before the text.

Alternately, if you are creating your own icon Webfont you will want to use the Unicode Private Use area to include glyphs in your font.

```
.icon-twitter::before { content: "/eo4o"; }
```

This has the same effect as the code above—adding the Twitter glyph—but, if for some reason the CSS does not load, the icon simply appears as a blank space rather than as a "t", and the user will see the icon label.

1 6: Now it's time to add the HTML code that will be used to display your icon.

```
<i              class="icon-twitter">              <span
class="hide">Twitter</span> </i>
```

We used an i and span tags in this example, which have no specific semantic meaning, so are safe to reuse for this generic case.

For example, if we look at the example, a typical social footer might look like <div id="footerSocial"> <a href="http://www.twitter.com/"><img src="twitter.png"></a> </div> could be replaced with:

```
<ul id="footerSocial"> <a href="http://www.twit-
ter.com/" class="icon-twitter">
<li class="hide">Twitter</li>

</a> </ul>
```

And then style as desired.

STYLING WEBFONT ICONS

Once created, Webfont icons are fully styleable with standard CSS and can be re-styled using CSS pseudo-classes such as :hover, :active, and :focus. There are a lot of ideas that you can bring to bear on styling Webfont icons; the sky is really the limit.

One limitation we noticed, and cannot seem to find a solution for, is that you cannot apply CSS transitions to any ::before or ::after object on the page.

See the Pen Styling Webfont Icons by Jason Cranford Teague (@jasonspeaking) on CodePen to test this code. Try hovering over the icons, or click the "CSS" or "HTML" tabs to see the working code.

FINDING WEBFONT ICONS OR MAKE YOUR OWN

The obvious question is "Where do I get the icon Webfont?" Although there are plenty of free and for-purchase icon Webfonts out there, the best solution is to create your own custom set using the free online IcoMoon app. You can choose from hundreds of different free icons or pay a small fee for access to a couple of thousand more.

IcoMoon allows you to create your own unique Webfont icon set and even add your own self-created glyphs.

What makes IcoMoon a fine app for Webfont icons is that it lets you build your own custom font from icons provided by IcoMoon or by uploading your own SVG files, a format that can be exported from Adobe Illustrator and most other vector editing programs.

ICON TAGS?

The idea of using fonts for icons is not a completely new one, but suffered from a lack of fonts to choose. An excellent tool like Ico-Moon, however, makes using fonts for icons a reality. With the growing popularity of Webfonts in general, This is a technique likely to quickly replace CSS sprites as the accepted method for adding iconography in UI design.

Still, there is something missing right now in Web standards that might makeWebfont icons more useful and effective. The W3C needs to add icon and icon label tags to the HTML standard to give the icons a semantic home. In the meantime, we'll have to make do with the more anonymous i and span tags.

SVG OR WEBFONTS

A positive reason for using a Webfont is the ability to use many of the CSS effects discussed in this book, and apply them to your icons, including drop shadows, blurs, gradients, outer glows and more. SVGs, on the other hand allow for many colors and gradients in your design, but this increases the icon's file size. Color thus becomes a negative for a Webfont, as its glyph is inherently a single specified color.

Last but not least are speed and download issues. Unless preloaded, each individual SVG icon will be a separate HTTP request. while a Webfont caches once, and can be used in its character set's entirety.

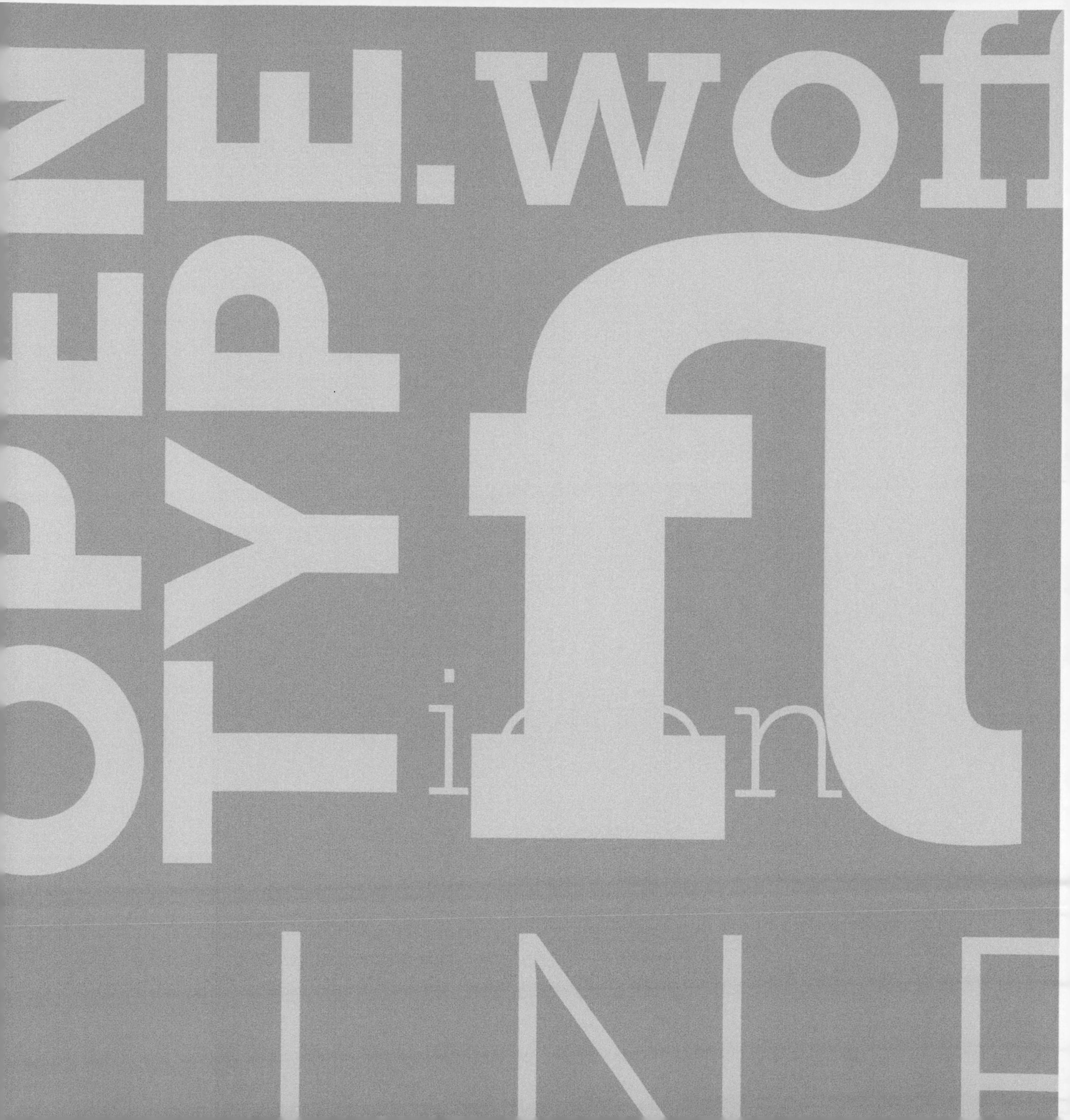
OPEN
TYPE.woff

HIERARCHY

9

The Grid is a tool for creating order, and creating order is typography.

— Wim Crouwel

We have interior structures called skeletons; they help keep us upright, give us limbs that can bear weight, keep our brains protected and connect to our tendons and muscles. Likewise, graphic design can rely on a similar theoretical structure called a grid. This grid gives us a predictable place to hold body copy, images, headlines and more.

This grid doesn't have to be as restrictive as it sounds; for example, you can create a three-column system, which allows for the merger of two columns on either the right or the left. A nice visual tension can also be created by merging two columns, insetting a photo sized to the width of one column and wrapping body copy around the image, creating a visual oasis in a dry, text-heavy layout.

abcdefghijklmnopqrstuvwxyz
LEAGUE GOTHIC

DO NOT DESIGN BY DEFAULT

When you talk, you modulate the tone of voice you choose for different audiences. Your voice and cadence will alter, depending on your intended audience. If you are talking to your boss, your voice will (hopefully) sound very different than if you were talking to your lover, even if the words are the same. Whether you adjust your voice for formal, informal, humorous, serious, sensuous, or angry tone will inform your audience about the meaning of your words.

Many Web designers allow the default values imposed by the browsers or perceived limitations dictate the voice of their designs and dictate their scale and rhythm, usually not well. It's like talking to everybody you know in exactly the same voice. Take control of your message.

RESET THE BROWSER DEFAULTS AND SET YOUR OWN GLOBAL STYLES

Although there is some technical debate over exactly how you should reset styles and which styles should be reset, as designers, we recommend resetting all typographic and spacing styles and then setting your own defaults. Beyond not allowing the browser to determine your page styles, another good argument for resetting styles is that different browsers will have slightly different values, especially for margins, padding, and font sizes and some browsers will include borders where others may not. Resetting the styles gives all of the browsers you will be dealing with the same baseline.

The easiest way to reset styles is with the universal selector and set the default styles you want applied to all tags:

```
* { margin: 0;

    padding: 0;

    border: 0;

    outline: 0;
```

This is a quick way to get the most important styles reset, but has one drawback, Internet Explorer 6 does not recognize the universal selector. If you are concerned about supporting IE6, you will want to include all of the HTML tags in the selector list. The advantage of using the universal selector is that it will always apply itself to new HTMl tags as they become available.

COMPOSE WITH A SCALE TO CREATE A TYPOGRAPHIC HIERARCHY

When scanning a Web page for information, the human eye looks for areas of contrast and areas of consistency. Too much consistency leads to a monotonous design while too much contrast leads to chaotic noise. One way to balance the contrast and consistency is to create a regular typographical hierarchy, where type fluidly scales from the top level (level 1 heading) into the body content (paragraphs).

The scale you choose is up to you, but keep it consistent and easy to remember. You may want to scale based on doubling 2's (2, 4, 8, 16) or multiples of 3 (3, 6, 9, 12, 16) or multiples of 5 (5, 10, 15, 20). These values should inform not only your font sizes, but margins, padding, and widths as well. Applying ems to scale allows you to create a relative scale that can then be controlled at the top level by setting the font size in the body tag.

One issue to overcome is the inconsistency of browsers in re-sizing fonts relatively, as some fonts will exaggerate the size changes more than others. One way to alleviate this issue is to simply set the font size of the body tag to 100%, which indicates that all tags should base their relative size on the browser's default font size.

```
body { font-size: 100%; }
```

Let's assume a default font size of 16 px (the default on most browsers). and you want a paragraph font size of 12 px. You can quickly create a scale, simple by using ems to scale the base font size up or down from there. For lower level headers, which are rarely used, you can use different styles, weights, or caps to differentiate them in the hierarchy.

MAKE LINKS CLEAR, NOT CLUTTERED

The default style for hypertext links on the Web is underlined, and this is the style that many readers have become accustomed to scanning for. Unfortunately, underlines do not contrast with the text, adding visual noise to the very elements they are meant to highlight. Additionally, since not all links are created equal, underlining all links—even those in navigation and controls—diminishes the overall typographic contrast of a page.

There is, however, a better way to underline links than using the underline style. Adding a border to the bottom of a link gives you an underline that is more controllable. Start by turning underlining off in all links on your page:

```
a { color: rgb(0,0,255);
```

If you really need a link type to be underlined, add it back on a case by case basis—for example, links in paragraphs—and use the border-bottom property instead. This lets you create a controlled underline:

```
p a:line { border-bottom: 1px solid rgb(153,153,255); }
```

```
p a:visited { border-bottom: 1px solid rgb(204,204,255); }
```

```
p a:link { border-bottom: 1px dotted rgb(153,153,255); }
```

```
p a:active { border-bottom: 1px solid rgb(255,0,0); }
```

FROM BOX TO GRID

Grids are time-honored methods for achieving regular structure and consistency on a page and between pages. For typography, the grid becomes important when considering the right font sizes for the space available. As mentioned in chapter 4, the readability of your layout is partially dependent on not allowing columns to stretch too wide or condense too small.

For Web design, the grid is not only useful; it is the default way that the page is naturally structured. While print designers can easily create elements of any 2-dimensional shape, every element in a Web page created using HTML tags has an intrinsic box around it. Although non-rectangular shapes can be placed within, the basic element shape will always be a rectangle. These rectangular boxes naturally lend themselves to creating solid layout grids.

However, Web design presents a problem not encountered in print because of the unpredictable nature of where the content will be displayed. Most Web designers will attempt to define a fixed width for columns, but as screens grow larger, adapting to this variable environment becomes more imperative.

STRUCTURE YOUR PAGE BY USE

There are a variety of methods for structuring a Web page grid, but given that HTML 5 will soon become the default mark-up language, we recommend mirroring its nomenclature, even if we can't use its exact code yet. One of the most significant improvements over previous mark-up languages is the addition of new structural elements that will greatly enhance the semantic philosophy behind Web mark-up. Here's a quick run-down of some of the key structural elements:

- Header: Pretty obvious, but can be used for page headers, section headers, article headers, or aside headers

- Navigation: Could be included independently or as part of the header and/or footer

- Section: Defines the main parts of the page, generally containing articles

- Article: An individual blog entry or blog entry abstract

- Aside: Used for support content on a page, such as related links, secondary navigation, and, of course, ads

- Footer: Similar to the header, it can be placed at the bottoms of other elements

Begin your grid by adding HTML tags with classes that identify the various sectors of your layout grid by their use within the design. We also recommend adding a surrounding parent element called **page**, which is used to control the overall width of the content area.

Once your basic structure is in place, you will use CSS to set your page and column widths, either using a fixed width for precise widths or variable width for fluid widths.

```
<html>

<head><title>FWT</title></head>

<body>

</div id="page">

<div class="header">

<div class="navigation"></div>

</div>

<div class="section">

<div class="article">

<div class="header"></div>

</div>
```

USE FIXED WIDTH FOR PRECISE GRIDS

Most Web designs make use of a fixed width page, generally centered in the browser window. Although standards have changed over the years, a content area width of 920 to 980 px is considered standard, assuming that the majority of monitors have a width of 1024 px or more. This provides comfortable spacing for most (but not all) people reading the page.

To set the page width, set the width of the page selector to the desired width; we'll use 960 px as an example. You could then calculate exact pixel widths for each column based on the formula presented in chapter 4, but we recommend setting column widths for sections and asides as percentages (including a percentage margin on section), as this will allow you to change the page width without having to recalculate the column widths:

```
.page {    width: 960px;


          margin: 10px auto; }

.section {  float: left;


          width: 50%;
```

The aside columns will be about 224 px and the central section column will be 480 px and the gutter between will be about 15 px. Notice that this only adds up to 958px, leaving an extra 2 pixels unaccounted for. These will be to the right of the page, but I it's good to leave a few pixels of breathing room in the design to account for rounding errors and different browser quirks. We've also added the auto margin to center the page.

USE VARIABLE WIDTHS FOR FLUID GRIDS

Although fixed widths are popular, consider an alternative—using CSS to create a column width range. Although a screen size of 1024 px is currently considered to be the smallest size, there are plenty of readers who may still have smaller screens and many more who simply don't keep their browsers open to full screen.

We would never recommend allowing columns to stretch unimpeded across an entire screen since after a point the width will reduce the readability of text. Likewise, columns can only get so thin before they become useless for reading text, and a horizontal scroll would then actually be preferred. However, there is a wide range of widths between these two extremes.

For optimal reading using a base font size of 16 px, the range in size for the central column should be somewhere between 400 px (16 × 25) and 530 px (16 × 33). Since we are setting the width of the page, we need to multiply this by a factor of two, since the central column is half the width of the page, giving us a range of 800 px to 1060 px—a healthy range. To set this range, we will rely on the min/max CSS properties:

```
.page {    min-width: 800px;

           max-width: 1060px;

           _width: 920px;

           padding: 0 1.5%;

           margin: 10px auto; }
```

The page will now stretch and contract to optimize to the reader's screen, without diminishing the readability. This code also accommodates readers using Internet Explorer 6, which does not recognize the min/max properties. Adding a fixed width with an underscore before it, is a quick hack to make sure that only IE6 sees it.

BODY COPY

This may be one of the most important typographic decisions that you make for your type stack. The body copy face should be easy to read, so consider a family with a generous x-height. People have an easier time reading copy when the lower case is on the larger side. Another decision is choosing sans serif or serif. We prefer sans serif faces because of their clean geometry. Some believe serifs help the reader by connecting letter forms to create words. Ultimately the decision involves style and preference.

OPENING GRAPH

There are many approaches to opening your site's body copy with panache. Some treatments include looser letter spacing, generous line heights, bumped up font size or even a font weight that is a hair heavier. Drop caps are another time tested treatment, (think of illuminated manuscripts) used throughout history to direct the reader's eye and give a little variation to body copy. This can be achieved with the first character tag.

INDENTS

Indents provide a visual cue to help the reader digest your copy easier. They can also aid in making your page lengths more compact. A common way to separate paragraphs is to insert a return between each paragraph which can eat up inches of space. Indents can replace this formatting and save you a line for every paragraph.

PARAGRAPH

Paragraphs can be formatted in many ways, rag right, rag left, centered and justified. The latter should be avoided because it is more than likely to create white rivers of space flowing up and down your page in a rather annoying way. Setting borders and padding can customize a paragraph's look.

OVERHANGING PUNCTUATION

Hanging punctuation pushes quotes and several other punctuation marks outside the paragraph's margin, vertically aligning the first character with the rest of the paragraph. This is achieved by using the hanging-punctuation tag. When setting copy in all caps, an opening cap, a slightly larger character, may be a great way to attract the eye without going overboard with more ornate effects.

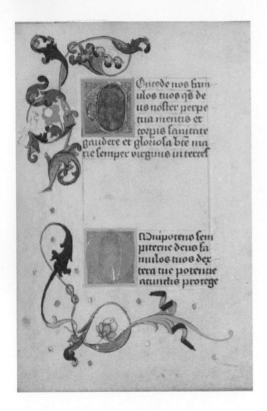

OPENING CAP

The initial letter form of a chapter is sized in relationship to the rest of the text. Medieval manuscripts routinely used this decorative treatment. Opening caps are a great way to illustrate your copy.

PARAGRAPH MARKER (¶)

A paragraph marker, also known as a Pilcrow, is a special character that marks a new paragraph, typically in a long flowing section of copy. The Pilcrow looks like a horizontally flipped P with two vertical strokes. The code for this character is ¶.

SECTION MARKER (§)

The section marker is often used in legal documents, and looks like two vertically stacked Ss. This symbol is used when referencing a certain section of legal text, such as a regulation. The code for the section marker is §.

NAVIGATION AND CONTROLS

Your site's navigation is one of its most important elements. Navigation should be clean, easy to see, and interact with. It should be as streamlined as possible. With so many hover events available now, your visitors will appreciate a judicious use of blurs and glows. The next chapter discusses iconography, which can get mixed into your navigation palette. We prefer avoiding underlined links in navigation, because it clutters the site's canvas. The navigational elements are obviously hot, so why be redundant?

Navigation should also be hierarchical if second tier links are required. This can be determined by doing a bit of site architecture before the design process begins, laying out what are second and third level links.

We prefer selecting a typeface, weight, or width for the navigation that is somewhat different from content font, just to clearly separate the navigational elements from the site's content. This practice is commonly called type pairing.

The advantage of using Webfont icons is accessibility. Webfont icons can be used in place of HTML text. The trick is to hide the HTML text from human users, replacing it with the icon using CSS, but allowing it to be displayed for screen readers and search engines.

GUIDING THE READER'S EYE

Visitors to your site will depend on your typographical prowess to make their visits memorable and easy. You should never create any roadblocks that could slow access to your information. Such roadblocks can include long column widths and letter spacing. Keep your column widths narrow enough so reader's eyes do not lose their place. Loose letterspacing can hamper readability by making words look disjointed and too spread out.

Letter spacing that is too tight can create dark masses of letter forms that don't allow the eye to get a grasp on a word.

RISK OF POOR TYPOGRAPHY

Poor typography won't place anyone in harm's way, but will create a mood that isn't welcoming to the reader. This could result in poor site statistics, abandoned shopping carts (on commerce sites), complaints, lost sales and general confusion.

To put it simply, the risk is a negative view of your or your client's site that could permanently damage your brand's reputation.

BALANCING READABILITY AND RETENTION

Designers often sacrifice style for readability, but sometimes a message is stronger and more impactful when you do the opposite. Your readers may well retain information if they have to work a little to digest it. Stacking words in interesting ways, adding angles, or drawing attention to specific keywords are good starting points for experimentation.

Editorial designers will often take over a whole spread with large images, large headlines, and blocks of body copy to create a high impact reading experience. You can bring this approach to the Web by overlapping images with text, with or without transparent overlap. This is also a great way to break out of your grid for an occassional design alternative.

CONTRASTING TYPE

Think in terms of weight, width, stroke ,and typeface categories. All of these, which we discussed earlier in this book, can add contrast to your typography. This creates visual rhythm, draws the readers through the pages, and leaves them wanting more. Contrast doesn't have to be limited to typeface weight. Colors and tonalities can play a huge role in drawing attention to headlines. A headline set at 30% of your color will recede and become more of a supporting character in your typography.

TYPOGRAPHY AT HAND

As more people access the Internet via mobile devices, it make senses to start considering a mobile version when you begin a design project. This is where your font choices play an integral role in your brand. To ease readability, you should avoid background colors, and heavy use of photography. Pay close attention to positive and negative space, because this will help the user read the copy quickly.

One issue you should remember is that mobile means on-the-go, so people may be reading your text outdoors in the glaring sun. I find that text set in midtones can be difficult to read, and adjusting your screen's brightness can almost make the text disappear. High contrast is key.

Column widths should be on the narrow side, and the text should be rag right. There is consensus that a line of copy shouldn't contain over 40 characters. We did some character counting on numerous text-heavy mobile sites and 30 characters per line seemed to create the most legible text and caused the least eye strain. Lines set with 35 to 40 characters per line created fatigue rapidly.

We can now revisit the discussion on sans versus serif. We find that the geometry of grotesque typefaces like Helvetica and Akzidenz to be the most legible. The generous negative space, uniformity of stroke weight,s and generous widths help readers quickly read the copy.

If you set your desktop site's body copy at either 14 or 16 pixels, and your headline (H1) to 44 to 46, you should rethink the relationship of your mobile site's headline sizes. You can keep the body copy the same, but bump your top headline down around 28 to 30 pixels, incrementally working your way down for H2 & H3. Keeping the desktop sizing would create cumbersome and heavy-handed headers on mobile devices, making many words loners, sitting solo on single lines.

VISUAL HIERARCHY

Headline size and contrast can also aid in moving the eye throughout your design. Bold headlines set in a face that varies from the body copy or bold text can draw attention to key paragraphs and new articles and items. The density of color, hue and saturation can also play a pivotal role in drawing the reader's attention throughout the layout. There are many resource books on color theory that go into depth about color's psychological effects.

LAYOUT GRIDS

If cement and rebar are the essentials of a building's construction, the grid is the skeleton for your design. Laying out grids can resolve many design issues you could encounter down the road. Traditional publications are almost entirely based on grids. There is no reason why we shouldn't bring this print approach to the Web. It assists the readers, by training their eyes where to go.

Many times, the kind of client you have or the content that you design for can dictate your grid solution. You may need a three column magazine-ike grid solution for a text-heavy educational site. A fashion or travel site might require an editorial solution to accommodate large images that span the browser's window. .

Faucibus et Orci ac Alique

Lorem ipsum dolor sit amet, consectetur adipiscing elit. Curabitur dolor nunc, lacinia sit amet interdum aliquam, dapibus in urna. Interdum et malesuada fames ac ante ipsum primis in faucibus. Cras id bibendum ligula. Donec felis nunc, cursus ut porttitor a, sollicitudin vel dolor. Duis ut libero sed risus sollicitudin aliquam. Aenean. Maecenas tincidunt erat sed erat

To aid readability, set your copy flush left, and size your font keeping lines around 30 characters per line.

SCRIPT
MONOSPACE
HUMANIST
RETRO

X

GEOMET

FIXED WI

AP

GHT

RIC

TH

true type flavor

PE
N

OPE

TY
PE

AFTERWORD

10

It is good taste, and good taste alone, that possesses the power to sterilize and is always the first handicap to any creative functioning.

Salvador Dali

As mentioned in the introduction, if you set type you are practicing the art of typography. The more you learn about readability, positive and negative space, typeface selection, color theory, type treatments, and font technologies, the more you can hone your skills and judiciously flex your creative muscles.

Remember, even an email communication can be finessed with fonts, links and navigational elements. The possibilities for applying typography are endless.

English is an evolving language and your knowledge base should be too. I highly recommend keeping an eye on the many design annuals that are available, because Web design can draw from other genres such as spatial design, broadcast and print. You will see fads come and go, but the time-tested approaches we covered will always hold true.

abcdefghijklmnopqrstuvwxyz
FANWOOD

APPENDICES

APPENDICES

APPENDIX A:
CSS FOR TYPOGRAPHY

TYPE SIZE

Common Type styling tags:

```
font-size: <absolute-size> | <relative-size> | <length> | <percentage>
```

```
font-size-adjust: none | <number>
```

TYPE WEIGHT AND STYLES

Within a typeface you will often find many variations on the common theme of the regular font—called Roman in some typefaces. The regular style is the default and is used if no other styles are specified.

ASIDE

The regular font—sometimes called Roman defines the standard default state of the font from which other weights and styles are determined—the upright non-bold version of the font as opposed to italic or oblique, for example.

WEIGHT

Many typefaces include one or more font weights that that are lighter or heavier than the default font, generally bold or black for darker fonts and light or ultralight for lighter fonts.

```
font-weight: normal | bold | bolder | lighter | 100 | 200 | 300 | 400 | 500 |
    600 | 700 | 800 | 900
```

STRETCH

Although weight determines the thickness of the overall stroke, stretch defines the font width relative to regular width. In order to work, the typeface will need to have fonts for each width. The following code shows common font weights.

```
font-stretch: normal | ultra-condensed | extra-condensed | condensed | semi-
    condensed | semi-expanded | expanded | extra-expanded | ultra-expanded
```

ITALICS AND OBLIQUES

Italics constitute a unique font, generally designed to look handwritten and script-like, generally slanted to the right. While commonly confused with italics, oblique fonts are angled versions of the Roman font, generally slanted 10 degrees to the right.

```
font-style: normal | italic | oblique
```

SMALL CAPS AND ALL CAPS

Use capital glyphs for lower case letters, adjusting the size for contrast. Small-caps are easy to synthesize for typefaces that don't include a specific version.

```
font-variation: normal | small-caps
```

APPENDIX B:
STYLISTIC ALTERNATIVES

UNDERLINE, OVERLINE, AND STRIKETHROUGH

Although they do not change the nature of the glyphs, underlining, overlining, and strikethrough are commonly used typography styles. Unfortunately, CSS has, until recently provided only limited control over the styling of text decoration, and I do not recommend using it at this time.

```
text-decoration: none | underline | overline | line-through
```

```
border-bottom: 1px solid red;
```

ASIDE

Currently only Firefox allows you to control the style and color of the line in text decoration, but this is a CSS property that all browsers will soon implement. In the meantime, the most common way to add a stylable underline to text is using border bottom, as explained in chapter 5.

TEXT SHADOW

Use this code to apply a drop shadow to selected text. This treatment pops yout typography off the page.

```
text-shadow: 6px 6px 4px rgba(150, 150, 150, 1);
```

```
text-shadow: none | <offset-x> <offset-y> <blur-radius> <color>
```

LETTERPRESS AND EMBOSS

This code mimics the the physical process of embossing paper, giving a raised effect to your typography.

```
#letterpress h1 {

  text-shadow: 0px 1px 1px #4d4d4d;

  color: #222;

  font: 80px 'LeagueGothicRegular';

}
```

```
#embossed h1 {

  text-shadow: -1px -1px 1px #fff, 1px 1px 1px #000;

  color: #9c8468;

  opacity: 0.3;

  font: 80px 'Museo700';

}
```

3D TEXT

The 3D effect gives your text either a plastic or metallic look. Adjust the numeric values to change colors for the highlights and shadows.

```
text-shadow: rgb(187, 187, 187) 0px 1px 0px,

  rgb(210, 210, 210) 0px 1px 0px,

  rgb(165, 165, 165) 0px 2px 0px,

  rgb(155, 155, 155) 0px 3px 0px,

  rgb(140, 140, 140) 0px 5px 0px,

  rgb(120, 120, 120) 0px 6px 0px,

  rgba(0, 0, 0, 0.199219) 0px 7px 1px,

  rgba(0, 0, 0, 0.296875) 0px 8px 6px;

Blurred Text

.blur-text

{

  color: transparent;

  text-shadow: 0 0 5px #000;

}
```

GLOWING TEXT

This treatment is similar to a drop shadow, it gives your typography a neon effect. This can create a rich hover effect for links.

```
text-shadow: 5px -1px 2px rgba(255, 255, 202, 1);
```

TRANSPARENT OVERLAP

This treatment is useful for adding text over photos and other design elements.

```
wrapper

{

    position: relative;

    display: inline-block; /* You could alternatively float the div,
     this is just to get it to fit the text width */

    z-index: 0;

}



.overlay

{

    position: absolute;
```

```
    top: 5

    bottom: 5;

    left: 5;

    right: 5;

    background: rgba(0, 0, 255, 0.5);

    z-index: -1;

}
```

GRADIENT TEXT

This treatment blends colors within each letter form. It can be a simple blend between black and white, or more complex involving multiple colors.

```
background: -webkit-linear-gradient(top, #878787, #000);
```

```
text-shadow: none | <offset-x> <offset-y> <blur-radius> <color>
```

APPENDIX C: TEXT SPACING

STYLING TEXT

Below are sample of tags used to format your paragraphs and typography. These samples cover indents, line height, justifaction and font selection.

```
text-indent: <length> | <percentage>
```

```
Word Spacing, Letter Spacing and Kerning
```

```
word-spacing: normal | <length>
```

```
letter-spacing: normal | <length>
```

```
Line Height (Leading)
```

```
Margins and Padding
```

```
Alignement
```

```
Justification
```

```
text-align: left | right | center | justify
```

```
text-align-last: auto | start | end | left | right | center | justify
```

Elipses

```
text-overflow: clip | ellipsis | <string>
```

OpenType

```
@font-face {

font-family: YourFontName;

src: url("path_to_otf_file/YourFontName.otf") format("opentype");

}
```

```
@font-face {

font-family: YourFontName;

font-weight: bold;

src: url("path_to_otf_file/YourFontName.otf") format("opentype");

}
```

grotesque

X CAP
HEIGHT
X
ETRIC

INDEX
THE NEW WEB TYPOGRAPHY

244

Printed and bound by CPI Group (UK) Ltd, Croydon, CR0 4YY

22/10/2024

01777530-0001